Light in the *Darkness*

Light in the Darkness

The Teachings of
Father James Keller, M.M.,
and The Christophers

Presented by

Father Jonathan Morris

OUR SUNDAY VISITOR PUBLISHING DIVISION
OUR SUNDAY VISITOR, INC.
HUNTINGTON, INDIANA 46750

The selections from the writings of Father James Keller, M.M., were taken from:

1. *Three Minutes a Day.* Garden City, NY: Doubleday & Company, copyright © 1949 by The Christophers, Inc.
2. *A Day at a Time.* Garden City, NY: Hanover House, copyright © 1957 by The Christophers, Inc.
3. *Three Minutes a Day,* Vol. 3. New York, NY: The Guild Press, Publishers, copyright © 1960 by The Christophers, Inc.

For permissions regarding Father Keller's writings, contact: The Christophers, Inc., 5 Hanover Square, 22nd Floor, New York, NY 10004; 1-212-759-4050; mail@christophers.org.

The Introduction and introductions to each chapter, copyright © 2014 by Father Jonathan Morris.

For permissions regarding the introductions, visit: www.osv.com/permissions. Our Sunday Visitor Publishing Division, Our Sunday Visitor, Inc., 200 Noll Plaza, Huntington, IN 46750; 1-800-348-2440.

ISBN: 978-1-61278-832-6 (Inventory No. T1639)
eISBN: 978-1-61278-377-2
LCCN: 2015936181

Cover design: Amanda Falk
Cover art: Shutterstock
Interior design: Dianne Nelson

PRINTED IN THE UNITED STATES OF AMERICA

Contents

Introduction

He was so right, and I wish I could go back in time to tell him how wrong I was.

It was a bitterly cold night in Harlem when I met this gentleman, a man whose name I am embarrassed to say I don't remember. Coming up from the subway that evening, I was in no mood for conversation. It couldn't have been past 5:00 p.m., but already it was mostly dark, one of those short days of the year that feel so very long.

The day at the office had been mostly disappointing. I wanted to get home, slump into the armchair, and zone out on ESPN. But I couldn't avoid him.

"Father, I need to talk to you," he forcefully blurted out, in Spanish, just loud enough and in the perfect tone to make sure everyone around us knew I heard him. He didn't bother to stand up or even move his head. Seated, with his back and head against a building, and with his forearms resting on his bent knees, he waited for me to come to him.

"How can I help you, sir?" I asked.

"Have a seat, Father, next to me."

He was sitting on a wet, partly shoveled sidewalk at Broadway and 116th Street.

"But, sir, I need to get home," I told him. "I've got someone waiting for me at the church. But … are you cold? I can send someone to get you some food and into a shelter for the night?"

"Have a seat, Father. By the way, your Spanish isn't too bad for a gringo."

I wasn't in the mood for compliments either.

"Father, you asked me how you could help me, and I'm telling you. Sit down next to me. I want to talk to you. I just got here on a bus from Chicago."

I knew the right thing to do, but convinced myself otherwise, with the perfect excuse. The safe thing to do — in a big city like New York, when it's dark and cold — is to tell the person you're in a hurry. After all, you never know....

But he didn't give me time to give a definitive "no." I'm sure he saw it coming.

"Father, here's what I would have told you if you had time. I just got word from home that my son got accepted here at Columbia University," pointing just to his left, to the main gates of the university at 116th and Broadway. "He'll be coming to New York City in six months. I haven't seen him in eight years since I left my country."

The glow of paternal pride on his face verified his authenticity.

"Oh my goodness," I responded. "Congratulations!"

At this point, I truly wanted to stay and get to know more, but I had painted myself so forcefully into a corner of busyness, of needing to go home, that I couldn't reverse my story with the slightest bit of grace.

I asked him his name, shook his hand firmly, and went on my way. He smiled graciously.

This man's story still haunts me. I blew it. I didn't have time to celebrate a miracle, or even to remember his name.

Looking back on it now, I'm certain this man wasn't homeless. And he wasn't cold. He had traveled across the country by bus in order to see, touch, and sit down on the rock-solid, hallowed ground of his son's future, of his whole family's future. For eight long years, he had toiled far from family so that one day his son might have a better life than him. That dream was coming to life right then and there, and he was eager to share the sacred moment with me. But I was busy.

I have no idea what I could have offered him had I taken the time to listen, but I know I missed a sacred moment, a God moment for me or for him, or for both. In this case, thankfully, the big story didn't depend on me. I was at the end of a long chain of sacred moments that were not missed, by a father and mother who gave up almost everything, including being together, for the sake of their son. And they changed the world, because they changed the world for him.

At the heart of such unconditional love is a conviction that you and I can make a difference. In the light of faith, that conviction is fortified by another conviction: that God has placed us on this earth to know him and love him and work with him to fulfill a mission of love toward all of God's children. Because God knew us before he formed us in our mother's womb, and wanted us, we know this mission is uniquely ours and nobody can do it for us.

Perhaps nobody has understood this life-changing truth of life-purpose better than Father James Keller, M.M. One day, in an empty, dark opera house, Father Keller witnessed the manager strike a match on his way to turn on the house lights. That little flame pierced the darkness and lit up the whole place! This was a moment of special grace in the life of this priest.

"What if," Father Keller thought, "what if all of us were to light a candle in this world of darkness. We could change the world." Father Keller made a decision there and then to dedicate the rest of his life to spreading the word that nobody is like you, and that you can make a difference for the good.

In 1945, he founded "The Christophers" organization — literally, from the Greek, meaning "Christ bearers." His original plan of being a Maryknoll missionary in China became instead missionary work to the whole world. Through radio, movies, writing, and networking, he spread the word that you and I, with the help of God's grace, can change the world. We can bring the light of Christ to an otherwise very dark world.

Father Keller died in 1977, but his message lives on in The Christophers, now an international family of individuals who take up the challenge to bring Christ into the world in whatever field they work, especially in those areas of great influence in our society, such as education, government, media, and entertainment. Father Keller wanted the organization to have very little structure so that every "Christopher" would take responsibility to change the world in his or her own way.

There are no membership applications, dues, or requirements. You know you are a "Christopher" if you are lighting a candle of love everywhere you go.

Over the last few years, I have come to know and love the Christophers' message for its wonderful simplicity and depth. Furthermore, I think it is remarkably timely as a spiritual antidote for the geopolitical and cultural crisis we now face.

Father Keller spoke often about the need to confront communism as an existential threat to humanity. He didn't take it lightly. He knew it would engulf the world if it were not stopped. And what was his solution? That little candle, again. The motto for the Christophers is the ancient Chinese proverb, "It's better to light one candle than to curse the darkness." Light can pierce and banish darkness. I don't think it was a coincidence that the movement that ultimately led to the fall of Soviet communism was the Solidarity workers' union that preached this same, positive truth. Through nonviolent, civil disobedience, Solidarity president Lech Walesa, with the support and leadership of St. John Paul II, and the political genius of Ronald Reagan and others, told the people they were right and their Soviet leaders were wrong. They told the growing membership that freedom, hope, and human rights were more powerful than the dictatorship of a few. In John Paul II's words, "Do not be afraid!" Wait it out. Light a candle. Be light in the darkness.

That strategy was victorious.

Twenty-five years later, the world is much smaller and, dare I say, the problems are much bigger. Many people whom I trust, who are older and wiser than I, believe that we are living in more dangerous and chaotic times than any other period in our country's history. I agree. In many ways the enemies of life and freedom today are even more vicious than the communist and Nazi regimes. While these fanatics hide behind pseudo-religious, Islamist ideologies, their actions have nothing to do with religion. They are brutal mass murderers who have silenced the voice of conscience and right reason. By their own admission, we know they will not stop until they have taken away our freedom or our lives.

The core of their power today is in the Middle East, but their digital and physical reach is now worldwide.

Besides the raw viciousness of these terrorists, what makes their threat so dangerous is that our arguments against them are weak. Secularization, on the one hand, and hyper-political partisanship, on the other, in the United States, Europe, and other Western countries have eroded our ability to coalesce around almost any costly cause of justice or even self-defense. If it comes with a price, we say it might not be worth it, right now. Secularization has made agreement on a basic moral code very difficult, and hyper-partisanship has transformed politics from the art of governance to a schoolyard rumble. In this atmosphere, our ability to explain to our citizens and to our enemies that freedom is worth fighting for is greatly diminished.

The answer? I think it's time for us to relearn from Father Keller how to light more candles. In this book, you will find a selection of my favorite writings of Father Keller, with a brief Scripture passage and a prayer added at the end of most entries. I have divided them into eight themes that I hope will stir our consciences and awaken in us a spiritual creativity to make a difference where we are right now, or where God is calling us to go. The chapters are: (1) A Sense of Purpose, (2) The Power of Love, (3) Sharing the Faith, (4) The Witness of Life, (5) Pray Always, (6) Becoming Like Christ, (7) Living as a Christian, and (8) Trusting God.

I have written an introduction to each chapter, sharing what I have taken away from the selection of writings that follows. I hope my thoughts open for you a window into the soul of a man who, many years ago, had much to say about today.

I dedicate this book to The Christophers on their seventieth anniversary, and to all the Christ-bearers who faithfully bring light into the darkness.

— FATHER JONATHAN MORRIS

Preface

This book aims to help people of every background and circumstance to add spiritual meaning and purpose to their daily lives. A particular objective is to remind persons like you that God has given *you* a special mission in life that He has assigned to no one else. It is up to you to discover what this mission is. If you think, pray, talk, and act with the conviction that you have a personal mission, you are bound to lead a worthwhile life and leave the world better than you found it.

A match struck in the darkened Metropolitan Opera House one winter morning in 1933 helped spark the idea that led to the founding of the Christopher movement twelve years later.

I was visiting the manager of the Metropolitan, and he invited me to see the interior of the opera house. When we entered the vast and empty auditorium, he asked me to wait in the rear while he went ahead to turn on the house lights.

In a second he had disappeared down the darkened aisle, and I could no longer follow his movements. For minutes I waited. Then suddenly, far up on the stage, a single flame flared as the manager lit a match to avoid stumbling over a prop or a piece of scenery. I will never forget the sight of that tiny flame as I stood in the last row of the orchestra.

Insignificant as the light of a single match was, it was enough to pierce the darkness. I could not help reflecting that all that was needed to banish the darkness completely was to multiply that flicker a million times. In a moment, the manager did just that. Crossing the stage he turned on all the switches, flooding the great opera house with light. Instantly the darkness was gone.

The power of that tiny pinpoint of light made a deep and lasting impression on me. It brought to mind ideas such as the following, which prepared the way for the Christopher movement:

- *Partaker in the Divine.* In every human being, Almighty God instills a small but important bit of divine power.
- *Every light in every human counts.* People will make great progress toward changing the world for the better as one person after another recognizes his power to light at least one tiny flame.
- *Each person is needed.* Many people will quickly abandon the feeling that they do not count and will lead forceful, worthwhile lives once they realize how much their pinpoint of light is needed. With it, they can pierce the gloom and raise the standards of public and private life.
- *A mission to fulfill.* Christ reminds us constantly that every person without exception has a mission to fulfill. That mission is to bring the light and warmth of His love to the world: "Your light must shine before others, that they may see your good deeds and glorify your heavenly Father" (Matthew 5:16).

Through the years, the simple objective of the Christopher movement has been to encourage millions of people to be "candle lighters" who will do something positive and constructive to right what is wrong with the world.

— FATHER JAMES KELLER, M.M.

– O N E –

A Sense of Purpose

I'm the third of seven children. I'm the only priest or nun in the family. Of the seven, I've heard my mom say that I was the least likely to have followed this path. I try not to take that personally — and honestly, that's not hard. I wouldn't have picked me either! Until shortly before I joined the seminary, I had no plans, thoughts, or even interest in being a priest. It just happened. At least that's how it felt at the time. My roommate in college was discerning a call to the priesthood and that intrigued me. With the goal of encouraging him, I set up and then accompanied him on visits to seminaries. He never joined, but I did. Then he asked me for permission to ask my girlfriend out on a date. Reluctantly, I gave him the okay, and they are now married with eight children. I've been blessed to give most of them their first Communion.

That might sound like a Cinderella story. It doesn't feel like one to me. And I'm pretty sure it doesn't feel like one for my roommate or his wife. We are all very happy with the path we have followed in answer to God's call, but it hasn't been easy. Cinderella stories on television and in sports start off hard and end in bliss. In the things that truly matter, no matter how we start off, bliss rarely shows up to stay. Instead, we struggle daily to live up to the lifelong choices we made long ago.

Does that sound too somber? I write it with a smile. I couldn't be happier that God called me to the life he has. It's not a happiness that comes from things in my life being easy or going my way. My joy comes from a deep confidence that God created me because he wanted me, no matter how things feel or go. He made me because he loved me even before my family knew me. He did this because he wanted also for me to know, love, and serve him in this life and to be with him forever in the next.

It would be fair to ask how I know this. I know it by faith. I know it too, at a different level, with my head and heart. By this I mean that I'm not torn between what my brain tells me and what my faith tells me. I believe it with all that I am. So much so, in fact, that I would bet my life on it. And I have.

This faith in God and his plan for me translates into a purpose-driven life, as my friend Pastor Rick Warren describes it. Father Keller saw in the Scriptures and in his Catholic faith that God is the author of our purpose. Jesus said that we are called to be light and seasoning for a dark and dull world. He invited us to "put out into the deep," to embark on the adventure of navigating salvation history for our own souls and for our neighbor. There was, perhaps, no other topic more dear to the heart of Father Keller than this conviction that you and I are created by God with a unique mission, and that if we discover our mission and work to fulfill it, we can change the world.

Do you know what your purpose is? Have you begun to fulfill your mission? Listen now to Father Keller's inspiring presentation of what God is calling you to do and be.

❧

— YOUR SPECIAL MISSION —

The expression, "man with a mission," appears occasionally in newspapers and magazine articles. It is a fit reference to a person who manages to keep his ideals high, his goal big, his vision clear, and who displays dogged determination in putting his convictions to work.

Such a person can do much to shape for the better the world in which he lives. Those without any purpose bigger than self rarely do anything worthwhile and usually turn out to be bores even to themselves.

We of the Christophers are constantly striving to arouse a sense of mission in millions of people. We try to remind one and all that God has assigned to each of them a special mission in life to perform.

Yes, you — whoever or wherever you are — have been personally given a particular role to play on the stage of life which has been given to no one else. God will provide every help to assist you in playing your role well. If you cooperate, the world itself will be better because you have been in it.

"You are the salt of the earth. But if salt loses its taste, with what can it be seasoned?"
Matthew 5:13

GUIDE ME, O DIVINE MASTER, TO FOLLOW THE PLAN
THAT YOU HAVE ASSIGNED TO ME.

– Into the Deep –

"Make no little plans. They have no magic to stir one's blood. Make big plans, aim high in hope and work" is the advice of one expert. You will never bring out the bit of greatness within you, if you set your sights low.

No matter how insignificant your role in life may seem, it is important. You have been delegated by God Almighty to help a world which too few are bothering to try and save. Evildoers are not content to defile the few. They have daring plans to debase and enslave all of mankind.

You are endowed with a capacity to embrace the whole world and everybody in it with your love. The more you develop your own great potential by setting big goals for yourself, the more meaning and purpose you will add to your life while benefiting countless others.

Christ told the fishermen He chose as His apostles to overcome their inclination to smallness. He bade them tackle the task of fishing in a daring way.

"Put out into deep water and lower your nets
for a catch."
Luke 5:4

LET ALL THAT I THINK, SAY, AND DO, O JESUS, BE MOTIVATED
BY DIVINE BIGNESS, NOT HUMAN SMALLNESS.

— FULLY ALIVE —

A man on a hiking trip through the Blue Ridge Mountains came to the top of a hill and saw, just below the crest, a small log cabin. Its aged owner was sitting in front of the door, smoking a corncob pipe, and when the traveler drew close enough he asked the old man patronizingly: "Lived here all your life?"

"Nope," the old mountaineer replied patiently. "Not yet."

However long or short it may be, there is time ahead for all of us to live our days with high purpose. When we lose this sense of purpose in life, we have lost an important part of life itself. Living each day fully is a vital part of being a Christopher.

"Do not worry about tomorrow; tomorrow
will take care of itself."
Matthew 6:34

O GOD, MAY I BE EVER AWARE THAT EACH DAY
IS A LIFETIME TO BE LIVED FOR YOU.

– It Can Be Done –

Two young men started an unusual hike from California to New York via the seashore.

Both hikers, in their early twenties, planned to follow the coastline of California from Los Angeles to the border of Mexico, then down the Peninsula of Lower California, and the west coast of Mexico and Guatemala to the Panama Canal.

After crossing the Canal Zone, their long detour would continue up the shore of the Caribbean to the Gulf of Mexico and the tip of Florida. The final leg of their journey should bring them up the eastern shore of the United States.

Why such a unique, arduous trek that will take eighteen months to complete? The young men simply replied: "To prove it can be done."

Once persons make up their minds to conquer an earthly goal, they will go to great lengths to achieve it. They can do the same for eternal goals. But they must first set their sights on heaven, and stir within themselves the determination and perseverance needed.

Think of what is above, not of what is on earth.
Colossians 3:2

Instill in me, O Lord, the tenacity
to win the crown of life.

– No Time to Lose –

The ship's chief engineer, coming down the companionway into the engine room, shouted: "How long have you been working in this compartment?"

The fireman, recently assigned to the crew, answered honestly: "Ever since I saw you coming down the ladder."

There is a constant temptation for all of us to "take it easy" until an emergency arises.

Often we tend to excuse our own spiritual idleness, putting off action to some future time which we imagine will be more opportune.

We are naturally inclined to believe that a kind of routine goodness is enough, and we postpone any really energetic spiritual activity. In actuality *every* day is the *right* day for spiritual labor — is the proper time for directing our moral energies toward our eternal goal. Indeed, there is no time to lose!

Behold, now is a very acceptable time; behold,
now is the day of salvation.
2 Corinthians 6:2

LORD CHRIST, GRANT THAT I MAY ALWAYS BE ALERT
TO SERVING YOU AND DOING GOOD TO OTHERS.

— PREPARING FOR ETERNITY —

Always popular are the following words, which are attributed to Stephen Grellet, French-born Quaker who died in New Jersey in 1855. For all of us Grellet's simple yet charged remarks can be a source of inspiration:

> I shall pass through this world but once.
> Any good thing I can do, or any kindness
> that I can show any human being, let me
> do it now and not defer it. For I shall not
> pass this way again.

How true these words are! And since we have but one brief "testing period" here in which to prepare for eternity, it behooves us not to waste or misuse it. The chance, once gone, will never be offered to us again.

> *Do not love the world or the things of the*
> *world. If anyone loves the world, the love of*
> *the Father is not in him....Yet the world and*
> *its enticement are passing away. But whoever*
> *does the will of God remains forever.*
> 1 John 2:15, 17

LORD, TEACH ME TO BE IN THE WORLD, NOT OF THE WORLD, AND
TEACH ME TO DO GOOD, THUS STORING UP TREASURES IN HEAVEN.

– AIM TO DO GOOD –

It's easy to slip into a passive or negative way of living. But those who smugly boast, "I've never done any harm to anyone," and think that's the peak of achievement really miss the big reason for living.

Nowhere in the Gospels does Our Lord advise us to take it easy.

Jesus repeatedly stresses that we should use our talent and not bury it by leading lives that are nothing better than harmless.

He emphasizes that our very salvation depends upon the positive good we do for others with the gifts He has entrusted to us.

Do good, He commands. Avoiding evil is not enough. Love your neighbor, He insists. That means far more than just tolerating or refraining from hurting others.

"Just so, your light must shine before others,
that they may see your good deeds and glorify
your heavenly Father."
Matthew 5:16

DEEPEN IN ME, O LORD, A YEARNING TO FILL MY LIFE WITH GOOD DEEDS, NOT MERELY TO AVOID HARM.

– The Wrong Way –

A tired passenger at the Los Angeles airport recently boarded what he thought was a Chicago-bound plane.

Dozing off immediately, he woke up several hours later and glanced out of the plane window. Instead of seeing the Rocky Mountains, he gaped in astonishment at the wide blue Pacific. The stewardess told him the plane was flying to Honolulu!

To make matters worse he couldn't even enjoy a day's stay in Hawaii because urgent business demanded his presence in Chicago. Two hours after landing in Honolulu, he was on a plane heading back for the mainland and Chicago.

Slight mistakes in these fast-moving times can cause havoc in more ways than one. The consequences of even the smallest oversight involving your soul may be far more serious than taking the wrong plane or train.

Check and double-check to make sure that your sense of purpose and direction is toward God, not away from Him, and you will save yourself much grief.

Steady my feet in accord with your promise;
do not let iniquity lead me.
Psalm 119:133

PROTECT ME FROM MY OWN CARELESSNESS, O LORD.

– TAKING INITIATIVE –

The word "pawn" is defined in Webster's dictionary as "the chessman of least value ... also, figuratively, an insignificant factor," as "a pawn in the political game."

Even if you are not a chess player, you probably have heard people refer to themselves as helpless pawns which don't count and can be pushed around without having anything to say about it.

But too often this is the fault of the individuals themselves. They lead completely passive lives, willing to be nudged here and there by the opinions and pressures of others. Because they are so negative, they often leave the way open for others to take advantage of them.

God made none of us pawns. Each one has a job and a responsibility toward helping the big world. God didn't create us to sit on the sidelines and wait for someone else to move us along. He wishes each of us to show initiative and daring — to make our influence for good felt in the mainstream of life. If we do, we'll be anything but pawns. We'll keep our individuality, and by the grace of God, we shall leave the world better than we found it.

> *"You are the light of the world. A city set on a*
> *mountain cannot be hidden."*
> Matthew 5:14

LET ME DARE TO TAKE INITIATIVE FOR YOUR SAKE, O LORD.

– WORKING WITH GOD –

"God gives the nuts, but He does not crack them," runs an old German proverb.

In short, the Lord wishes each of us to work with Him in solving problems, small and large.

By accepting this responsibility, you will —

1. Learn not only to think for yourself, but also how to put your original ideas to work.
2. Discover hidden talent that you never realized you possessed.
3. Become self-reliant when your own experiences prove that your contribution is needed.
4. Show more daring for good once you discover ways and means, on your own initiative, to solve problems affecting everybody.
5. Develop your imagination and enterprise each time you strive to be a "self-starter."
6. Enjoy the sense of personal fulfillment that the Lord promises to those who, while depending on Him, put to good use the reasonable independence which He expects each of us to show.

"Ask and it will be given to you; seek and you
will find; knock and the door will be opened to you."
Matthew 7:7

HELP ME, O DIVINE MASTER, TO FACE MY RESPONSIBILITIES,
NOT DODGE THEM.

− LIVE CREATIVELY −

Someone once asked Mallory, the famous climber who lost his life on Mount Everest, why he wanted to attempt to scale that mountain.

Mallory answered simply: "Because it is there."

The daring climber saw a challenge in the very existence of the uncharted peak, and something would not let him rest until he had attempted it.

Many of us would like to drift through life, taking it as it comes, following the easy path. But for others a challenge exists — the challenge to live creatively, to mold life into something worthwhile. Like the climber, they see the difficulty and the hardship, but they see also the reward: a deep sense of accomplishment — the sense the Christian has when he carries Christ up the steep slopes and keeps in sight the end of the climb — the peak of eternity.

... nor height, nor depth, nor any other
creature will be able to separate us from the
love of God in Christ Jesus our Lord.
Romans 8:39

LORD, TEACH ME NEVER TO TURN AWAY FROM THE CHALLENGE LIFE
OFFERS TO WIN SOULS BACK TO YOU.

– THE COST OF DISCIPLESHIP –

When you accept a position of responsibility, don't be surprised by the troubles, problems, disappointments, and misunderstandings that go with it. Such trials are the penalties of leadership.

Far from being disheartened by hardship, regard it as a badge of honor. It is usually the best possible proof that you are on the right track.

The Leader of Leaders constantly reminds all who would be effective Christ-bearers in His cause that they must earn their battle scars. "If anyone wishes to come after me, he must deny himself and take up his cross daily and follow me" (Luke 9:23).

Look beyond the heartaches and heartbreaks that you are bound to encounter. They are the lot of every worthwhile leader. Never forget that you are winning most while you seem to lose.

One day you will have the consolation of saying with St. Paul:

> *I have competed well; I have finished the race;*
> *I have kept the faith. From now on the crown*
> *of righteousness awaits me, which the Lord,*
> *the just judge, will award to me on that day.*
> 2 Timothy 4:7-8

HELP ME TO REALIZE THAT I AM WINNING WHILE I SEEM
TO BE LOSING, O MY SAVIOR.

— ENDLESS LOVE —

A ninety-nine-year-old doctor in Pennsylvania gave a forceful answer when asked why he did not retire after nearly seventy years of practice. "Who would take care of my patients?" Was his reply.

Declining a proposal to make his birthday a community celebration, the dedicated doctor, said to be the nation's oldest practicing physician, insisted on keeping his usual office hours.

Those who devote their time, talent, and energy to the service of others who are in physical, intellectual, or spiritual need enjoy life as few others do.

Seldom do they seek or feel the need of the pleasures and diversions which are almost a necessity for those who have occupations to which they give little of themselves.

Whatever your job in life may be, try to see in it countless opportunities to share the blessings that God has entrusted to you with as many people as you can — and for as long as you can.

Be on your guard, stand firm in the faith, be
courageous, be strong.
1 Corinthians 16:13

REMIND ME, O JESUS, THAT I HAVE ONLY A COMPARATIVELY
SHORT LIFE IN WHICH TO PREPARE FOR ETERNITY.

– A Big Vision –

Two men were working on a cathedral. One, a skilled artisan, cut the stone needed in the construction of the great building. But his gloomy, grouchy attitude plainly showed that his work meant little more to him than providing him with a livelihood.

The other man was just an unskilled laborer. His job was simply to carry the stones that the artisan prepared. But he went about his work with such zest and enthusiasm that a passerby asked him how he could be so happy doing such an ordinary task.

"How can I be so happy?" he exclaimed. "Why, man, I'm building a cathedral."

Greatness of outlook and purpose can inspire anyone to reach beyond the narrow confines of a kitchen, factory, or office and contribute to the common good of all.

God blesses bigness of vision. Those who truly strive, even in an insignificant way, to bring His love and truth to all men realize that they are truly trying to build a new world.

"Go into the whole world and proclaim the
gospel to every creature."
Mark 16:15

DEEPEN IN US, O HOLY SPIRIT, AN APPRECIATION OF HOW WE CAN
RISE TO GREATNESS THROUGH BIG VISION.

— WHERE AM I HEADED? —

"Where did we come from?" "Where do we go?" And in be-tween: "Why are we here?" The answer to these questions are at the heart of Eugene Vale's penetrating novel, *The Thirteenth Apostle.*

This provocative story dwells in a most engaging manner on the "mystery of our role on earth — the great questions at the beginning and end of our existence."

It is a gripping account of a search by an American consul, an artist, lost in the mountains of a small Caribbean country. The quest leads the consul into deep soul-searching. Readers find themselves confronted by the same eternal challenge "which can be pushed from our minds, but cannot be denied."

God made you to know Him and love Him in this world, and to be happy with Him for all eternity. The more fully you comprehend this divine purpose for your existence, the more meaning and nobility you will add to your own pilgrimage through life.

"In my Father's house there are many
dwelling places. If there were not, would I
have told you that I am going to prepare a
place for you? And if I go and prepare a place
for you, I will come back again and take you to
myself, so that where I am you also may be."
John 14:2-3

INSTILL IN ME, O HOLY SPIRIT, THAT DIVINE DISCONTENT
HERE BELOW THAT LEADS TO PERFECTION HEREAFTER.

The Power of Love

Have you heard St. Augustine's monumental spiritual advice: "Love God, and do what you will"? That sounds like Jesus, doesn't it? It's the Gospel in a nutshell. Think for a moment of Jesus' last two major discourses to his apostles before he was arrested and crucified, the Last Supper and then his "final discourse." Essentially, they are wildly loving pronouncements of love. Wildly loving, because Jesus doesn't speak in theory or with platitudes. He is telling his closest friends that the Christian love he is calling them to entails a willingness to live and die for your friend or enemy.

During the Last Supper, Jesus gives his apostles his body and his blood, a foretelling of the way he will die for them. And then in his "final discourse," as it is often called, Jesus tells them not to worry when he is gone because he will be with his Father and will send the Holy Spirit upon them. And then, he simply commands them to love one another.

I have been with a lot of people on their deathbed. Some of them have been beautiful deaths. A few of them have been terribly tragic. What has separated the two types of death is neither age nor expectation of death, but rather whether or not there was love, given and received, between the dying and the survivors, and ultimately between the dying and the author of life, God himself. Where there was love, there was beauty because there was peace. Where there was built-up anger and resentment, at the hour of death, there was only confusion and desperation.

How do we assure a life and death marked by love? The subsequent lines of St. Augustine's famous homily I quoted above are less well known, but equally as helpful: "If you keep silence, do it out of love. If you cry out, do it out of love. If you refrain from punishing, do it out of love."

This is the practical application of spirituality that Father Keller so loved. He was fascinated, not by love as a virtue but rather love as a life-transforming gift from God. He loved to talk about "the power of love," the power to transform our hearts and the world.

Dive now into his hope-filled and practical vision of a simple life of love.

❧

– LOVE IS ENOUGH –

There is an ancient tradition about the last days of John the Evangelist. He lived to a great age and became so feeble he had to be carried to the meetings of the faithful. There, because of his weakness, he was unable to deliver a long discourse; so at each gathering he simply repeated the words, "Little children, love one another."

The disciples, weary of hearing the same words over and over, asked him why he never said anything else. And to them John gave this answer. He said, in effect, it is the commandment of the Lord: "Do this alone and it is enough."

If we adhered to these words the difficulty and complexity of our daily lives would disappear. In this clear advice we have the solution to all the problems that create hatred and strife among nations.

So faith, hope, love remain, these three; but
the greatest of these is love.
1 Corinthians 13:13

O LORD, I LOVE YOU WITH ALL THAT I AM;
HELP ME TO LOVE MY NEIGHBOR.

– THE SECRET OF LOVE –

When he was conductor of the New York Philharmonic Orchestra, Artur Rodzinski said: "In our orchestra we have many nationalities, types, and temperaments. We have learned to forget individual likes, dislikes, and differences of temperament for the sake of music to which we have dedicated our lives. I often wonder if we could not solve the world's problems on a similar basis of harmony."

"Think what a single individual in a symphony orchestra can accomplish," the famous maestro continued, "by giving up his individual traits and ambitions in the service of music.... Suppose that in life you had the same all-embracing love for the whole of mankind and for your neighbor in particular. Only when every one of us and every nation learns the secret of love for all mankind will the world become a great orchestra, following the beat of the Greatest Conductor of all."

Not until all men look up to the "Greatest Conductor of all," giving Him their devotion and wholehearted love, will they learn the "secret of love for all mankind."

> *"You shall love the Lord, your God, with all*
> *your heart, with all your being, with all your strength,*
> *and with all your mind, and your*
> *neighbor as yourself."*
> Luke 10:27

O GOD, GRANT THAT MY LOVE FOR YOU MAY
OVERFLOW INTO LOVE OF OTHERS.

– Love Always Wins –

Napoleon, in his lonely exile on St. Helena, had much time for thought. And some of his reflections were highly interesting. This one, for instance:

> Alexander, Caesar, Charlemagne, and I founded great empires. But upon what did the creation of our genius depend? Upon force. Jesus alone founded his empire upon love, and to this very day millions would die for him.

Forcing none, Christ taught in a new way, the only one throughout history whose whole school and whole plan were founded on love. The world had never before heard of this love. And even now, twenty centuries later, more than half the world is still ignorant of it. Often Jesus seems to lose, but in reality He always wins — and always by love.

> *"I give you a new commandment: love one*
> *another. As I have loved you, so you also*
> *should love one another."*
> John 13:34

O God, I want to love you as you would have me love.

– ALL FOR THE LOVE OF GOD –

The Huron Indians, who occupied part of what is now New York State when it was still a wilderness, gave violent reception to some of the missioners from Europe who came among them. But to two of these missioners, Fathers Brébeuf and Lalemant, both Frenchmen, they paid a strange compliment indeed. After subjecting them to the most horrible tortures, they tore out their hearts, ate them, and drank their warm blood. Why? Because their courage so impressed them that they wished, by drinking their blood, to have instilled in them some of the bravery of the men they put to death.

What first moved the Hurons to treat these two as they did? It wasn't the courage of Brébeuf and Lalemant alone. It was the cumulative effect of the fortitude of those missioners who had gone before them … Isaac Jogues, René Goupil, and the rest. Their sufferings were almost unbelievable. They were beaten with knotted sticks, their hair, beards, fingernails were torn out, their fingers chewed off at the ends.

Yet they bore all this for love of God and the Indians, in whom they saw the image and likeness of God. From their sufferings came forth the flowering of faith. In death they were victorious. A powerful example to fortify Christophers when faced with suffering!

> *"Then they will hand you over to persecution,*
> *and they will kill you. You will be hated by all*
> *nations because of my name."*
> Matthew 24:9

WHATEVER COMES, LORD, I BEAR IT ALL FOR YOU AND WITH YOU.

– Love Without Limits –

A Christopher may be distinguished by love for all people. Most of us love "some of the people some of the time," but few of us love "all of the people all of the time." A dangerous trend is developing among Christians. They are beginning to hate, to return hatred for hatred. This method has never yet had lasting results with Christians or anti-Christians. Love, on the other hand, has made possible the very condition of Christian civilization that protects every individual from the evils that follow in the wake of hatred. We must remember that Christ died for *all* men, even those who crucified Him. He asked us to bring His love to "all men" of "all nations." Upon this basic principle rests the whole spirit of the Christopher.

The love of God has been poured out into our
hearts through the holy Spirit that has been
given to us.
Romans 5:5

O Holy Spirit, fill my heart with love for everyone I meet.

– Unconditional Love –

A wealthy young couple walked into a large orphanage one day to adopt two children. They gladly filled out forms and gave vital statistics, while the officials of the institution did their best to make the visitors comfortable.

Finally, the director, beaming with satisfaction, said: "Now we'll show you two of the nicest children in the orphanage."

The wife turned quickly and then remarked kindly but firmly: "Oh, please, no! We don't want the nicest children; we want two that nobody else would take."

We naturally choose to associate with people we like, those who are most congenial. But we are missing something important in life if we do not try to go beyond this limited circle. Every follower of Christ is entrusted with a portion of His love that he is expected to share with others, especially with those who have little of it and therefore need it most.

"For if you love those who love you,
what recompense will you have? Do not the tax
collectors do the same?"
Matthew 5:46

LORD, STRENGTHEN ME TO SHOW CONCERN FOR THOSE
WHO ARE FORGOTTEN BY OTHERS.

– Who Is My Neighbor? –

G. K. Chesterton was not merely joking when he wrote, "The Bible tells us to love our neighbors, and also to love our enemies; probably because they are generally the same people."

Sometimes when we hear that modern communications and transportation have brought people closer together, we forget that the worst wars in history have occurred in just this period of heightened contact.

The mere act of bringing people closer together in physical and intellectual contact will never of itself guarantee harmony. There must be, first of all, spiritual contact, a sharing in the same realization that we have all been created by the same Father and for the same purpose.

"But I say to you, love your enemies, and pray
for those who persecute you, that you may be
children of your heavenly Father, for he makes
his sun rise on the bad and the good, and
causes rain to fall on the just and the unjust."
Matthew 5:44-45

LORD, GIVE ME THE GRACE TO LOVE MY ENEMIES
AND PEOPLE I DO NOT LIKE.

– HATE THE SIN, LOVE THE SINNER –

An ancient anecdote about Mohammed illustrates an important rule of conduct: that we should not try to advance ourselves by deprecating others. The story goes like this:

A disciple came to Mohammed one morning and said, "Master, my six brothers are all asleep and I alone have remained awake to worship Allah."

Mohammed answered him: "And you had better been asleep, if your worship of Allah consists of accusations against your brothers."

Faultfinding and magnifying the mistakes of others are poor ways of changing the world for the better. Wrongdoing, of course, has to be identified, but means to correct it should always be positive and constructive, not negative and destructive.

A Christopher — a bearer of Christ — will detest the sin but not the sinner. He will advance the cause of justice and peace and truth, yet he will not do so at the expense of the feelings of others. Always his motto will be: "It's better to light one candle than to curse the darkness."

> *If anyone says, "I love God," but hates his*
> *brother, he is a liar; for whoever does not love*
> *a brother whom he has seen cannot love God*
> *whom he has not seen.*
> 1 John 4:20

GUIDE ME, O LORD, THAT I MAY NEVER STRIVE
TO RISE BY PUSHING OTHERS DOWN.

– DOING THE LOVING THING –

In La Rochefoucauld's *Maxims* there is one thought which is particularly worthy of reflection. It goes:

> However brilliant an action, it should not be esteemed great unless the result of a great motive.

Often we hear people say of someone: "He does so much." Yet this may not always be a compliment. While it is certain that idleness is a vice, it is not necessarily true that action is a virtue. The evildoers of the world are frequently all too active.

The best course is always to act from a motive we can be proud of. To perform a kindness out of love — Christ-like love — is the highest behavior. Just as God so loved the world that He gave His only Begotten Son to us to purchase our salvation, so should we be inspired in all our actions by love of Him. That is the Christopher purpose. That is the Christopher motive!

> *For the love of Christ impels us, once we have*
> *come to the conviction that one died for all;*
> *therefore, all have died.*
> 2 Corinthians 5:14

O LORD, MAY I ALWAYS DO ALL THINGS FOR LOVE OF YOU.

– THE LOVE PRESCRIPTION –

An eminent baby specialist had a standard treatment for frail newborn infants who failed to gain weight.

When he came to such a baby's chart during his rounds in the hospital, invariably he scrawled the following direction to the nurse in attendance: "This baby to be loved every three hours."

Not alone do newborn babies need affection. Doctors agree that many of our physical ills result from a feeling of insecurity or loneliness, of not being wanted. True of our bodily sicknesses, how much more true it is of our spiritual difficulties. Love of neighbor remains the best advice — both for our neighbor and for ourselves.

> *Let love be sincere; hate what is evil, hold on*
> *to what is good; love one another with mutual*
> *affection; anticipate one another in showing honor.*
> Romans 12:9-10

JESUS, TEACH ME TO LOVE EVEN YOUR LEAST WITH
THE SAME LOVE WITH WHICH YOU LOVE ME.

– A GENEROUS ACT OF LOVE –

In one of the battles of the Civil War when his army was suffering a severe defeat, General Lee rode over a section of the battlefield where the fighting had passed on. As he did so, a wounded Northern soldier in the spirit of defiance lifted his head and shouted: "Hurrah for the Union."

The soldier then expected to be shot, but instead Lee dismounted and said simply, "I'm sorry that you are so gravely wounded. I hope you may soon be well."

Afterward the soldier said: "That spirit broke my heart, and I cried myself to sleep."

Often others are hateful to us only because they expect unkindness and are anticipating it. When they receive instead a word or a gesture of friendship, they are defenseless and quickly ready to return the kindness they are given. Just as hatred breeds hatred, so love creates love.

Put on love, that is, the bond of perfection.
And let the peace of Christ control your
hearts, the peace into which you were also
called in one body.
Colossians 3:14-15

GIVE ME, LORD, AN UNDERSTANDING SYMPATHY
EVEN FOR THOSE WHO MISTAKENLY HATE THE TRUTH.

– A Sacrifice of Love –

A gallant jet fighter pilot stayed at the controls of his disabled plane till it crashed in San Diego, California, in order to prevent it from hitting a school with one thousand children.

Just before he met his death, this heroic twenty-one-year-old flier, Albert Hickman, of Sioux City, Iowa, frantically waved at the children who were eating lunch in the school playground, in a desperate effort to warn them to run.

Only God knows what thoughts raced through the mind of the brave young pilot during the last minute or so of his life.

The desire for self-preservation must have been compelling. But his love for others and his respect for the rights of helpless children were far more powerful.

Behind this noble self-sacrifice must have been long and deep convictions. Seldom does one rise to the heights of "greater love" unless it has been always a dominant factor in his life.

*"No one has greater love than this, to lay
down one's life for one's friends."*
John 15:13

LET ME SO FILL MY HEART WITH LOVE FOR OTHERS, O LORD, THAT I
WILL SUFFER MUCH IN ORDER TO HELP THEM.

– Doing Good –

A few summers ago I was in a group that went from Paris to the little town of Lisieux. Much of it was destroyed by the war, but not the convent where a little French girl had entered at fifteen and died at twenty-four: Thérèse of Lisieux, the Little Flower of Jesus. She, probably more than anyone else who has lived in our day, has reached millions simply by loving everybody the world over. In some mystic way they came to know of her, to feel sure that she cared for each of them individually.

Her whole secret is expressed in her own words inscribed above her tomb: "I would like to spend my heaven doing good on earth."

She understood the important difference between merely "*being*" good and "*doing*" good; between being just a "hearer" and not a "doer." And because she wanted to reach others with her love, the Lord blessed her. Once you start "*doing*" good, you deepen, strengthen, and increase your "*being*" good. You, too, will start to reach out in love to all men as far as you can. It may well be, then, that God will bless you as He has blessed Thérèse.

Be doers of the word and not hearers only.
James 1:22

LORD, HELP ME TO SPEND MY WHOLE LIFE ON EARTH
BRINGING YOU TO AS MANY AS I CAN.

– Hold Fast to Love –

Much attention is given to the wills of prominent people, to the distribution of their wealth and property. But one of the most meaningful testaments we know of is that of a New York woman who left her children a valuable piece of advice in addition to her worldly goods. These are the last lines of her will:

> Love one another. Hold fast to that whether you under-
> stand one another or not, and remember nothing really
> matters except being kind to one another in the name
> of Christ and to all the world as far as you can reach.

"Hold fast" … it is interesting to note the woman's choice of words. She knew well that it wasn't an easy task she had bequeathed her heirs. And yet, she told her children not only to be kind to one another but to "all the world as far as you can reach." This farsighted woman certainly practiced the second great commandment:

> *Above all, let your love for one another be*
> *intense, because love covers a multitude of sins.*
> 1 Peter 4:8

Help us, O Lord, to hold fast to our aim to bring the love of Christ to all, as far as we can reach.

THREE

Sharing the Faith

Not long ago I was at a friend's home to watch a Sunday afternoon football game. He and his wife have five children and live in a New York City apartment. Needless to say, when everyone is home, the quarters are tight ... everyone is very present! That's why I was surprised not to see their oldest son, a precocious eight-year-old who is the life of the party. Ten minutes into my visit, Jack came out of the children's bedroom with his head down, blue marker and paper in hand. Normally he would have come straight to me to say hello. Not today. Instead he walked over to his mom, and without lifting his head, he handed her the half sheet of paper.

"Would you mind if I let Father Jonathan read it with me?" his mom asked, graciously. "It's okay," he responded. She read it out loud in a soft voice: "Dear Mom, I am sorry for having thrown a tantrum. It's because you weren't listening to me."

I held back a smile. Mom was less impressed.

"Close, Jack, but go back and try again."

From his reaction, it was clear he knew what wasn't quite right about his prose. Five minutes later he emerged again from the bedroom, marker and paper in hand.

"Dearest Mom," it read. "I'm sorry for having thrown a tantrum. It was because I was tired."

I was curious as to what his mom would say this time. It sounded pretty good to me, for an eight-year-old. Mom knew better.

"Jack, you are getting closer, which means I know that you know what's wrong with this one too."

Jack wasn't happy, but he didn't complain. Back to the room he went. It couldn't have been more than three minutes when he returned, this time with a very different demeanor, head raised and a half-smile on his face.

"Dear Mom, I'm sorry for having thrown a tantrum." Period.

What a powerful witness this couple gave me of transmitting their faith to their children. It was just another day of family life, but for Jack, he was learning the value of truth, humility, and repentance. There's a reason why the Church refers to the family as "the domestic church"! The family is the most natural place for us to live and share our faith. For many reasons, this doesn't always happen, and more and more young people are growing up with no religious education at all. Does this mean we should be indifferent to the sad reality of so many people never coming to know and love God? Absolutely not!

Here again, Father Keller was ahead of his time. In the pages that follow, you will read the passion with which Father Keller writes about sharing our faith. You will also feel his compassion and mercy. He looks to Scripture and then makes God's command to us to "go and make disciples of all men" a doable project. Much like Pope Francis in our day, Father Keller didn't see any purpose of beating people over the head with the Bible or proselytizing for the sake of increasing our numbers. For him, sharing his faith was passing on a gift he freely received from God, and for others.

∼

– Launch Out into the Deep –

Constantly aware that their Divine Master had left in their hands the duty of spreading His Word, the early Christians remembered His urging: "Go into the world ... to all men!" (see Mark 16:15). When they felt timid they remembered His words, "Launch out into the deep!" (see Luke 5:4). Over and over again He had exhorted them to "go into the highways and byways" (see Luke 14:23).

No wonder these early Christians left behind them marvelous results, visible today: they replaced brutality with gentleness and love, brought ideals of justice into government and business. Men and women began to recognize the sacred nobility of human life, the sanctity of marriage and the home.

If this handful of early Christians, with every possible obstacle in their path, could eventually remake a civilization even more rotten and brutal than ours, is there any excuse for us today to feel discouraged? If we work half as hard as they did, if we, too, become Christ-bearers, we should be able to restore truth to an unbalanced world.

"... and the truth will set you free."
John 8:32

I LOVE YOU, LORD, AND I AM DETERMINED TO MAKE YOUR PRESENCE FELT IN THE WORLD.

— Perseverant Christ-Bearers —

The part that women played on the first Easter day is a great tribute to their devotion, trustworthiness, and singleness of purpose.

First of all, Mary Magdalene and a few other loyal women were the only ones to go to the tomb of the crucified Savior.

Secondly, they were entrusted with the first mission to be given to anyone after Christ had risen. The angel commissioned them with this all-important assignment: "Go quickly and tell his disciples, 'He has been raised from the dead' "(Matthew 28:7).

Finally, they patiently persisted in trying to convince the unbelieving apostles that Christ had actually risen from the dead. The Gospel narrative sums up in a few words the resistance of the disciples: "… but their story seemed like nonsense and they did not believe them" (Luke 24:11).

The example of these devoted women can encourage you in fulfilling your God-given mission in life. If you, too, are alert, loyal, and persevering, you are bound to do great good.

Grant me the grace, O Risen Savior, of being
an instrument of your peace and love.

— Beyond Ourselves —

Some time ago I took a trip on the Hudson and Manhattan Transit System. During the journey, not being familiar with the names of the various stops (there are only a half dozen), I turned to the man next to me and asked: "Can you tell me the name of this station?"

"Sorry, I can't," the stranger replied. "I've been riding this line for fifteen years and I only know two stops: where I get on and where I get off."

There are many people who limit their horizons as did this traveler. They concern themselves with saving their own souls — which is of first importance — but fail to concern themselves with trying to save the souls of others — which, in God's eyes, they are duty bound to do. They think merely in terms of two "stops": their origin and last destiny. They overlook the "stations" along the way, crowded with human beings who are searching for God.

Being a bearer of Christ not only means knowing where you come from and where you are going. It also means helping others find their way to an eternity of peace with God in heaven.

*"What I say to you in the darkness, speak in
the light; what you hear whispered, proclaim
on the housetops."*
Matthew 10:27

COME, HOLY SPIRIT, AND HELP ME SHARE THE FAITH
WITH MY FAMILY, FRIENDS, AND NEIGHBORS.

– Win People, Not Arguments –

Not long ago a young businessman left a very important conference after engaging for more than an hour in a heated debate over policy. As he entered his own office, he muttered in a boastful tone to his secretary, "Well, I guess I won that argument!"

Personal triumph seems to have been the source of this young man's happiness. He seems to have been less interested in helping others to see the truth than in pushing himself. His was the shallow "pride of being right," not the joy of helping others better to understand the truth.

The true Christopher is far less interested in winning a debate, in forcing someone to admit defeat, than in helping him to arrive at the truth. One seldom wins people by argument, but only by love, which aims at supplying what may be lacking in others.

Death and life are in the power of the tongue.
Proverbs 18:21

LORD, TAKE FROM ME THE "PRIDE OF BEING RIGHT,"
AND GIVE ME THE LOVE OF SHARING WITH OTHERS
THE TRUTH YOU HAVE ENTRUSTED TO ME.

– DEAD RIGHT, BUT DEAD WRONG –

Did you ever run across the following jingle?

Here lies the body of Jim Jay
Who died defending his right of way.
He was right, dead right as he sped along
But he's just as dead as if he were wrong.

In driving, as well as in many other circumstances of life, well-intentioned people often do more harm than good by being a bit too stubborn.

By exaggerating a point of view, often good in itself, one individual can antagonize and hurt family, friends, fellow workers, fellow drivers and everyone else. In organizations much good is frequently prevented because a few members persist in making unreasonable demands.

Make at least one little step toward lasting peace in the world by showing more consideration for the just rights of others. This can be done without watering down one's principles. It takes a little more time and patience, yes. But if you are truly interested in the greater good to be achieved, you will gladly accommodate yourself to others and thus avoid the fate of Jim Jay who is "just as dead as if he were wrong."

"Should anyone press you into service for one
mile, go with him for two miles."
Matthew 5:41

GRANT ME THE UNDERSTANDING PATIENCE, O LORD,
TO SHOW CONSIDERATION FOR THE OTHER PERSON'S
POINT OF VIEW.

— GENTLE PERSUASION —

In Holman Hunt's painting "The Light of the World," Christ is shown in a garden at midnight, holding a lantern in His left hand. With His right hand He is knocking on a heavily paneled door.

When the painting was unveiled, a critic remarked to the painter, "Mr. Hunt, the work is unfinished. There is no handle on the door."

"That," Hunt answered, "is the door to the human heart. It can be opened only from the inside."

God does not force Himself or His law upon us; we are free to deny Him. But we are reminded constantly of God's love and desire to come to us.

It is most important for all Christophers to follow this same respectful approach in reaching others. Be ever ready to share Christ's truth, but gently offer it to others. You can't force it on them.

"Behold, I stand at the door and knock. If
anyone hears my voice and opens the door,
[then] I will enter his house and dine with him,
and he with me."
Revelation 3:20

LORD, HELP ME ALWAYS TO SPEAK TO OTHERS ABOUT YOU
WITH GENTLENESS AND UNDERSTANDING.

– WHERE ARE YOU GOING? –

An American riding on a train in northern China found the behavior of a native vendor extremely interesting. There was nothing unusual about the man's appearance, but he seemed to be having an odd effect on the other passengers. He leaned over each of them in turn, extolling his wares, but didn't make one sale. Despite that, he would ask each person some further question, and the answer invariably was a startled look on the passenger's face.

Finally the American's curiosity led him to call the vendor over and ask him what it was that upset the travelers.

"Well," the native explained, "I ask them: 'Where are you going?' and they usually answer, naming this city or that.

"But then I tell them that isn't what I meant — that what I meant was: 'Where are you going when you die?'

"It seems to make every one of them stop and think!"

This is, admittedly, an odd way of being an apostle, a Christopher, and helping others for eternity — but it still is a way!

> *"Therefore, stay awake, for you know neither*
> *the day nor the hour."*
> Matthew 25:13

PRAY THAT YOU MAY BECOME MORE AND MORE AWARE
OF THE ETERNITY OF REWARD OR PUNISHMENT WHICH
AWAITS YOU, AND THAT YOU MAY PASS THIS AWARENESS
ON TO OTHERS.

– The Lesson of Love –

Dante, that great-hearted, large-minded exemplar of all that was bright and good in medieval Christendom, once described the purpose of his writing in these beautiful words: "I am the man who, when Love lectures in the heart, takes notes, and then re-tells the lessons to the rest of men."

Whether we are writers, teachers, government employees, trade unionists, businessmen or wage-earners, housewives or students at school, we can — each one of us — reflect in our own relationships with others some small portion of the purpose and depth of understanding of the divine which made Dante the man he was.

We can listen to the lessons which the God Who is Love teaches us through religion and prayer, through friends, through nature, through books, and make it our most joyous aim in life to bring that lesson to others.

"But now ask the beasts to teach you, the birds
of the air to tell you;
Or speak to the earth to instruct you, and the
fish of the sea to inform you.
Which of all these does not know that the hand
of God has done this?"
Job 12:7-9

LORD, TEACH ME YOUR LESSON OF LOVE AND ENABLE ME
TO RETELL IT TO THE REST OF MEN.

— Ways to Hand on the Faith —

There are various ways by which a Christopher can pass on to others the principles that guide his life and give it eternal purpose:

1. *By listening to those in trouble.* Many who are confused, in sorrow, in doubt, or discouraged want to talk to someone. That may be the very moment in their lives when they will listen to the real Truth. A kind word, a helping hand, listening to those in trouble may often be the means of bringing the peace of Christ into their lives.

2. *By interest in those far from Christ.* The very purpose of Christ's coming to earth was to win sinners. He asked those who would be Christophers to do the same. Rather than devote attention to "saving the saved," one of the Christopher's chief objectives should be to reach those who are farthest from Christ and therefore need Him most.

3. *By informing those who know not.* Most of the hundred millions in our country who are not reached by anyone in the name of Christ actually hunger for His teachings. Too few Christians are interested in them. Many who have no religion feel that Christianity does not want them, because it makes so little attempt to reach them.

> *And how can they believe in him of whom they*
> *have not heard? And how can they hear*
> *without someone to preach?*
> Romans 10:14

LORD, HELP ME TO LOVE THOSE WHO DO NOT KNOW YOU
AND THOSE WHOM IT IS DIFFICULT TO LIKE.

– Sharpen Your Communication Skills –

Too few of us know how to express ourselves adequately, and because of this we fail to spread the good ideas entrusted to us by God.

Because of such neglect, the positions of influence often go by default into the hands of those who are determined to mislead rather than lead.

Take advantage of every opportunity to communicate ideas. These few tips may help:

- Remember your importance as a connecting link between God and others. You may be the transmitter of divine truth to many a person who would never hear it except for you.
- Acquaint yourself with some fundamentals of public speaking and effective writing.
- Above all else, deepen your convictions — your love of God and people. You will never stimulate others to action if words come only from your lips, not from your heart. The Apostle Paul warns:

> *If I speak in human and angelic tongues but do*
> *not have love, I am a resounding gong or a*
> *clashing cymbal.*
> 1 Corinthians 13:1

THANK YOU, O HOLY SPIRIT, FOR THE PRIVILEGE OF BEING
A DISTRIBUTOR OF YOUR DIVINE TRUTH.

– Seize the Day –

The Metropolitan Museum of Art some time ago held a display of contemporary art at which $52,000 was awarded to American sculptors, painters, and artists in allied fields.

The award for the best painting went to the canvas of an Illinois artist. It was described as "a macabre, detailed work showing a closed door bearing a funeral wreath." Equally striking was the work's title: *That Which I Should Have Done I Did Not Do.*

Few of us could win an award for painting. Many of us would not even attempt to produce a work of art. Yet there are so many things in life that we *would* do, we say, "if only there were time."

And so the years slip by and, with them, all our opportunities for serving others, for doing good personally to those who need help. Each day presents thousands of opportunities, large and small, for reaching out to the world as far as we can. We have only to grasp the chance. Any day is a good day to start, especially today!

> *"We have to do the works of the one who sent*
> *me while it is day. Night is coming when no*
> *one can work."*
> John 9:4

PRAY THAT YOU MAY DO SOME GOOD TO EACH PERSON
YOU MEET TODAY.

– TAKE CHANCES –

In a small country hotel in the West there is an old sign tacked on the dingy wall behind the front desk. It reads: "No checks cashed. Not even good ones."

The proprietor was overcautious. As a result, he lost many a customer.

There is such a thing as being too careful. Those who are afraid of making even a slight mistake often end up by doing nothing at all. They have so much fear of evil that they don't do any good. They are the "neither-nor" type.

The Lord told us to take a chance — to "launch out into the deep" (see Luke 5:4) — to get into the thick of things. You may suffer — you may even drown by going into the deep to help others. But it's so much better to go down in defeat trying to do the right thing than to stay on shore with no other thought except to protect yourself.

To be any kind of a Christ-bearer, you must be willing to take chances for the Lord's sake.

*"Children! be courageous and strong in
keeping the law, for by it you shall be
honored."*
1 Maccabees 2:64

O LORD, HELP ME TO DO ALL I CAN FOR YOUR SAKE,
REGARDLESS OF THE COST TO ME.

– No Excuses –

Christ avoided no one. He talked not only to his disciples and well-wishers, but to unbelievers, to those who distrusted him, and even to scoffers. He is seen at a marriage feast, in the market place, among the rich, and among the poor. He built always on the material that was at hand. He took people as they were.

Reading the New Testament one is inevitably impressed by one thing: a conviction that every human being, every human situation has its own character and its own value from Christ's point of view.

It is easy to talk with our friends, with those who understand us and think as we do. The real test comes when we must go among strangers and especially into situations which are hostile.

What a temptation there is to let the opportunity slip by! To say to ourselves, "This isn't the right moment," or "There's nobody here who wants to listen to me." Every moment is the "right" one; every person deserves to be told the Truth.

> *But they went forth and preached everywhere,*
> *while the Lord worked with them and*
> *confirmed the word through*
> *accompanying signs.*
> Mark 16:20

O HOLY SPIRIT, MAKE ME ALERT TO THOSE
WHO NEED TO HEAR THE GOOD NEWS,
AND GIVE ME THE CONFIDENCE TO SPEAK WITH THEM.

– Giving Sight to the Blind –

During an annual drive in New York for contributions for the blind, store windows on Fifth Avenue were ablaze with posters. But there was one sign — a very simple one — that seemed to arrest most of the passersby. It read: "You can see. Will you help those who cannot?"

There is no one of us who would not, if it were in his power, restore a blind man's sight. Yet each of us must know many people who are spiritually blinded by prejudice, hatred, or ignorance. They need our help, and we can give it. Even if our own spiritual sight is not yet perfect, we can still lead those others toward the eternal light.

When he became aware of this he said to them,
"Why do you conclude that it is because you
have no bread? Do you not yet understand or
comprehend? Are your hearts hardened? Do
you have eyes and not see, ears and not hear?
And do you not remember...?"
Mark 8:17-18

GRANT, O LORD, THAT AS WE HAVE BEEN ENABLED BY YOUR GRACE
TO SEE YOUR BEAUTY AND YOUR TRUTH, SO MAY WE HELP
THOSE WHO CANNOT SEE.

– Second Chances –

In the Academy at Florence one of the great Italian master-pieces displayed is Michelangelo's statue *David*. Yearly thousands of people admire this early example of the great master's work, unaware that the huge block of stone from which the figure was hewn has a curious history.

At first an inferior artist began to work on it, but through lack of skill, he succeeded only in hacking and marring the marble. Then the rulers of Florence called on the young Michelangelo, who created a lasting work of art.

There is no one so ruined that he is undeserving of a second chance. As the true artist saw in the shapeless mass of stone the outline of his masterpiece, so God sees in the lowest of the low that unextinguished spark of goodness and humanity which can be his salvation.

All of us can do the same, looking at everyone in a *creative*, not destructive, spirit. God will guide us in the good work of restoring what was lost, of giving life to what was spiritually dead.

"For God so loved the world that he gave his only Son, so that everyone who believes in him might not perish but might have eternal life."
John 3:16

O LORD, AS YOU HAVE SO OFTEN GIVEN ME A SECOND CHANCE,
GRANT THAT I MAY ALWAYS HELP OTHERS TO HAVE
THEIR SECOND CHANCE.

– THE POWER OF FRIENDLINESS –

Christ showed special regard for those whom we are inclined to shun. Zacchaeus is a good example of our Lord's solicitude. In a few hundred words Luke tells the story of this publican, who climbed up a sycamore tree out of curiosity to see Jesus.

Jesus astonished the crowd and Zacchaeus himself by saying: "Zacchaeus, come down quickly, for today I must stay at your house" (Luke 19:5). Moved by this unexpected gesture of Christ, the rich sinner took immediate steps to make full amends to all he had wronged.

Often a surprise act of generosity or friendliness will melt the most frozen heart or move the most hardened sinner. All of us have known people whom others found terrifying and austere, who were, we discovered for ourselves, only shy and afraid of being rejected. Real Christ-like affection is the surest letter of introduction, the always-welcome gift, the most valid passport.

"This is how all will know that you are
my disciples, if you have love for one another."
John 13:35

LORD, GIVE ME YOUR EYES TO SEE THE GOOD IN EVERYONE I MEET.

– A Quick Change –

There were a lot of factors against Zacchaeus. He was rich, a sinner, and, worst of all, he was a publican, a tax-gatherer. Yet he climbed a tree to see Christ; out of idle interest, true — but interest, nevertheless.

When Christ singled out Zacchaeus and sought his hospitality, the crowd murmured that He was consorting with a sinner. They openly disapproved of such an action: they wanted Him for *themselves*, as have many good people down through the centuries. But Our Lord went to Zacchaeus's house, despite the censure of the throng.

The result? Zacchaeus immediately caught the spirit of Christ and learned of Him the meaning of commutative justice. "Behold, half of my possessions, Lord," he exclaimed, "I shall give to the poor, and if I have extorted anything from anyone I shall repay it four times over" (Luke 19:8).

Our Lord's loving solicitude prepared the way for such a change of heart. Love accomplished in a matter of minutes what cold logic might never have succeeded in accomplishing.

> *"For the Son of Man has come to seek and to*
> *save what was lost."*
> Luke 19:10

LORD, FILL MY HEART WITH A GENEROUS LOVE
THAT WILL DRAW PEOPLE TO YOU.

– Comforting the Lonely –

In Chicago, not long ago, a thirty-five-year-old woman committed suicide. To one who didn't know her well, she would have seemed to have everything anyone could want out of life: comfort, social position, and the rest. Yet she often complained of the loneliness that had confronted her in childhood and had followed her all through her life.

Shortly before her death she spoke of the emptiness of her existence and referred to her life as a "horrible mess."

Our hearts should go out to people like this. More often than not, their whole outlook would have been healthy and normal if someone had showed a bit of interest in them in the name of Christ. But left alone — trained only to concentrate on self — the qualities God put in them never got a chance to develop. With no proper outlet, stagnation and decay set in: pent-up energy often goes haywire and an "explosion" inevitably is the result. Yet many a human tragedy could be averted by a little thoughtful solicitude on the part of some Christopher.

Why are you downcast, my soul,
why do you groan within me?
Wait for God, for I shall again praise him,
my savior and my God.
Psalm 42:12

GOD, GRANT THAT I MAY TAKE EVERY OPPORTUNITY
TO BRING THE JOY OF CHRIST INTO THE LIVES OF THOSE
WHO ARE FRUSTRATED AND DEPRESSED.

— You Can Be a Christ-Bearer —

Back in the third century, a giant son of a heathen ruler longed to serve someone greater than himself. First he enlisted in the ranks of a great king, and then of the Devil. But he was disillusioned in both.

Hearing finally that Christ was the King of Kings, he desired to serve Him above all others. He discovered he could do this by helping those in need. One way to do this, he thought, would be to carry travelers across a dangerous stream nearby.

One day, while this powerful man was bearing a small child across the river, he found his burden so backbreaking that he could scarcely reach the other bank. On looking up, he was surprised to find that he was actually bearing the Christ Child, holding the world in His hands.

Without realizing it, this stalwart man had become a Christ-bearer — a Christopher. Since that time he has been known far and wide as St. Christopher.

You, too, can be a Christopher. You — whoever you are — can do something to carry the love and truth of Christ into the heart of twentieth-century life.

> *"Go, therefore, and make disciples of all nations."*
> Matthew 28:19

LORD, GIVE ME THE STRENGTH AND CONFIDENCE
TO SERVE YOU AS A CHRIST-BEARER.

The Witness of Life

Good and true concepts, like the ones I am trying to pass along to you in this book, are important because they clean out our brain. Like a back closet that ends up with cobwebs when left unattended, our minds are subject to the lies and half-truths that secular culture weaves about the meaning of life and the source of happiness. Before we can act with courage against such a strong current of worldly values, we need this kind of regular washing of our hearts and, yes, our brains.

But I have seen in my own pursuit of doing God's will that concepts alone aren't always enough to get me to change my ways. I might know what I should do, but I don't always do it. It is seeing someone else do what I know I should do, especially in the face of obstacles — their witness — that moves me to make the tough decisions.

This year I went to Mexico City to visit the shrine of Our Lady of Guadalupe. I had known of the great devotion in Mexico, the United States, and many other parts of the world to this particular apparition of Mary. I had seen the striking image of her that was left miraculously on the cloak of Juan Diego when Mary appeared to him in 1531. But those were concepts to me. It was interesting, but it wasn't transformative. It wasn't until going to the shrine and seeing the faith and devotion of millions of people who walk days and in some cases weeks to come to the shrine that I fell in love with Our Lady of Guadalupe. I fell in love with her because I experienced the love of others for her; I heard their stories of favors received; I watched in awe as the young and old alike walked on their knees for miles as a way to say thank you to God and to his mother Mary. That is witness. That changes lives.

In the following selections from Father Keller's writings, he teaches us to re-think the best way to pass on our faith to others. That includes passing on our faith to our children, or family members who don't share our beliefs. There is no better pedagogy, he would say, than the silent witness of a Christian life.

❧

— DIVINE YEAST —

A little cake of yeast can teach a big lesson.

As soon as it is added to a pan of dough, the bit of leaven goes right to work. Slowly but surely, it penetrates every segment of the mass, causing it to rise and expand.

You can help permeate the whole of modern life with the love and truth of Christ if you think of yourself as a bit of "divine yeast."

You can do something that nobody else can accomplish to raise the standards of the great spheres of influence that affect the destiny of everyone for time and eternity. Show a special interest in improving government, education, labor relations, and writing, including both literature, and entertainment.

To have a leavening effect upon the world in which you live, you must do as Christ said and go into the midst of things.

Unless you reach out to the marketplace through prayer, word, and deed, you may have no greater influence on life than a cake of yeast on the shelf in its paper wrapper.

"I tell you, everyone who acknowledges me
before others the Son of Man will acknowledge
before the angels of God."
Luke 12:8

DEEPEN IN ME, O SAVIOR, A CONSUMING DESIRE
TO LEAVEN THE WORLD WITH YOUR LOVE AND TRUTH.

– THE BASIC TRUTHS –

It has been the consistent practice of the atheists and the materialists to concentrate on undermining, ridiculing, or eliminating the *basic truths of religion* that remind mankind of the necessity of keeping everything God-centered. They know that once these go, all the derivative truths and practices that depend on these primary principles become virtually meaningless. So first, last, and always they center their attack on *Number One Truths*. It seems ordinary common sense, therefore, to take a tip from them and focus particular attention, far and wide, on the following ten great fundamentals which they strive incessantly to destroy:

1. The fact of a personal God, Who has created and spoken to the world;
2. Jesus Christ, true God and true man;
3. The Ten Commandments;
4. The sacred character of the individual;
5. The sanctity of the lifelong marriage bond;
6. The sanctity of the home as the basic unit of the whole human family;
7. The human rights of every person as coming from God, not from the State;
8. The right, based on human nature, to possess private property, with its consequent obligation to society;
9. Due respect for domestic, civil, and religious authority;
10. Judgment after death.

"You will know the truth, and the truth will set you free."
John 8:32

LORD, TEACH ME NOT TO KEEP THE PRIMARY TRUTHS TO MYSELF,
BUT TO DO MY BEST TO SHARE THEM WITH OTHERS
WHO KNOW THEM NOT.

– The Witness of Life –

The word "Christopher" is derived from the Greek *Christophoros,* which means "Christ-bearer." With the aim of restoring to all phases of life, public and private, divine truth and human integrity, the Christopher goes into the marketplace, into a job of his own choosing, without fanfare or flag-waving. He is not out to do anything sensational. His task is to insist on truth where others are insisting on falsehood. Where there is hate, he brings in love; where there is darkness, he carries light.

The Christopher emphasizes the normal rather than the abnormal. Nothing remarkable may ever be required of him beyond a generous spirit of daring.

He expects to do the usual, not the unusual; the ordinary, not the extraordinary. He knows that while the steady fulfillment of duty often involves monotony and drudgery, yet his continuing sacrifice is ever lightened by a driving purpose. The most trivial and tiresome task achieves significance when done for Christ, Who said:

"For my yoke is easy, and my burden light."
Matthew 11:30

LORD, HELP ME TO ACCOMPLISH GREAT THINGS FOR YOU BY DOING
THE LITTLE THINGS THAT LIE AT HAND.

– A Wake-Up Call –

A Seattle lawyer once interrupted his lengthy cross-examination of a witness and exclaimed, "Your Honor, one of the jurors is asleep."

"You put him to sleep," replied the judge. "Suppose you wake him up."

Every single one of us has played some part in the moral bankruptcy of the modern world — most frequently by what we are *not* doing for the common good of all.

Surely if we have contributed to the deterioration which we see on all sides — positively or through our sins of omission — it is only fair that we should now do our level best to reverse this trend.

There is still time. If enough persons with sound values go into the thick of things and strive to restore the peace of Christ and His wisdom to mankind, we may yet rescue our civilization from destruction.

Become sober as you ought and stop sinning.
For some have no knowledge of God; I say
this to your shame.
1 Corinthians 15:34

LORD, HELP ME TO DO MY SHARE TO RESTORE CHRIST
TO THE MARKETPLACE, AND HELP ME TO INFLUENCE
OTHERS TO DO THE SAME.

– PUTTING MAN RIGHT –

An overworked businessman came home one night, hoping to read the evening paper in peace and quiet. But his six-year-old son wanted attention. Tearing into small pieces a part of the paper which had a map of the world on one side of it and the picture of a man on the other, the father gave it to his son and told him to put the map back together again.

In ten minutes his son returned, the task completed. Since the boy had no idea of geography, the businessman wondered how he had done so well.

"All I did," said the boy, "was to put the man right. When I did that, the world came out right!"

The big battle of our day is over man — *the worth of man.* It is a battle for man's soul. Are you doing as much to reach all men with the truth of their divine origin as are those who deny God and are striving to eliminate all knowledge of Him from the face of the earth?

> *For our struggle is not with flesh and blood*
> *but with the principalities, with the powers,*
> *with the world rulers of this present darkness,*
> *with the evil spirits in the heavens.*
> Ephesians 6:12

LORD, HELP ME TO DO MY PART IN THE BATTLE FOR MAN'S SOUL.

– ZEALOUS SERVICE –

The life of the soldier attracted Ignatius Loyola when he was quite young. His chief aim was to achieve military glory. But on the twentieth of May 1521 Ignatius was seriously wounded in battle. During his convalescence he resolved to dedicate his life thenceforth to the greater glory of God.

To this end he began a long period of preparation — some eleven years in all. And so earnest was he to fit himself for the task of serving his fellow man for love of God that he humbled himself to the extent of studying Latin in the company of small boys in order to advance his knowledge.

Even though he was thirty-three years old when he began his training, he did not excuse himself from the effort by saying that he was too old. He knew that nothing could excuse him from doing the work he was called to do. As he himself put it:

> The most precious crown is reserved in heaven for those who do all that they do as zealously as possible: for to do good deeds is not enough by itself: we must do them well.

LORD, GRANT THAT I MAY DO SOMETHING
WORTHWHILE FOR YOU, AND THAT I MAY DO IT WELL.

— FAITH-FILLED TEACHERS —

The first president of King's College, now Columbia University, the Reverend Dr. Samuel Johnson, an Episcopal minister, made every effort to build the institution upon a recognition of that cornerstone without which no solid educational edifice can be erected: In a public notice which he composed and published in 1754, he stated:

> The chief thing that is aimed at in this college is to teach and engage the children to know God in Jesus Christ and to love and serve Him in all Sobriety, Godliness, and Righteousness of Life with a perfect Heart and a willing Mind.

What a refreshing change for the better would take place in our educational system if only a few thousand teachers would make every effort to uphold this ideal — at least as a minimum. Each of us can make this possible by encouraging those with sound principles to go into the field of education.

The LORD has rewarded me with lips,
with a tongue for praising him.
Sirach 51:22

O HOLY SPIRIT, GUIDE FAITHFUL MEN AND WOMEN WHO BELIEVE IN
YOU TO CHOOSE TO INFLUENCE THE WORLD AS TEACHERS.

– TEACHING THE TRUTH –

When Daniel Webster, the great statesman and orator, spoke at Faneuil Hall, Boston, in 1852, he underlined the great service anyone renders who dedicates himself to teaching God's truth:

> If we work upon marble, it will perish; if we work on brass, time will efface it. If we rear temples, they will crumble to dust. But if we work on men's immortal minds, if we impress on them high principles, the just fear of God and love for their fellow-men, we engrave on those tablets something, which no time can efface, and which will brighten and brighten to all eternity.

Those who take up a career in teaching, with a sense of devotion and dedication that makes seemingly great difficulties become very small indeed, clearly recognize the privilege of being God's instruments in bringing His Truth even to the least of men. For them, *purpose makes the difference!*

"I am the way and the truth and the life."
John 14:6

O LORD, SEND TEACHERS, SWORN TO YOUR TRUTH,
INTO EVERY CLASSROOM IN OUR LAND
AND OVER THE WORLD.

– GOD AND COUNTRY –

At the south end of the Tidal Basin in Washington, D.C., stands the classic memorial to Thomas Jefferson. On a panel near the statue we find in Jefferson's words a forceful and explicit warning that removing God from this country will destroy it. Here he says:

> God who gave us life gave us liberty. Can the liberties of a nation be secure when we have removed a conviction that these liberties are the gift of God? Indeed I tremble for my country when I reflect that God is just, that His justice cannot sleep forever.

More than lip service is needed to keep alive in our national life a deep conviction that our freedom is God-given. It is so easy to take for granted that the blessing of liberty will continue to be ours even though we make little if any effort to merit it.

Those who are fired with a love of God and country should above all others make it their business to apply moral principles to government, education, and the other great spheres of influence. Neglect or failure to do so may mean abandoning the field to those who would eliminate the very Author of our liberty from the face of the earth.

> *"We have to do the works of the one who sent*
> *me while it is day. Night is coming when*
> *no one can work."*
> John 9:4

HELP ME, O LORD, TO DO MY PART TO RESTORE YOUR TRUTH
TO THE WHOLE OF LIFE.

– A GOVERNMENT DEPENDING ON GOD –

Basing their authority on God, our Founding Fathers drew up one of the noblest of all documents. In this brief charter they might have referred only *once* to the Creator. But to underline fundamental truths, which they feared others might discard, they wove into the Declaration of Independence four significant sentences, two at the beginning and two at the end. Each specifically affirms the dependence of every human being on God:

1. The first reads: *"When in the course of human events, it becomes necessary for one people … to assume … the separate and equal station to which the laws of nature and of nature's God entitle them…."* Our forefathers emphasized that the natural law itself depends on God.
2. The second is equally positive: *"We hold these truths to be self-evident, that all men … are endowed by their Creator with certain unalienable rights."*
3. Toward the end of the document the authors appeal *"to the Supreme Judge of the world"* for the rectitude of their intentions.
4. The Declaration closes *"… with a firm reliance on the protection of divine Providence, we mutually pledge to each other our lives, our fortunes, and our sacred honor."*

"God of my ancestors, Lord of mercy,
you who have made all things by your word
And in your wisdom have established humankind
… to govern the world in holiness and righteousness."
Wisdom 9:1–3

LORD, GRANT THAT WE AND OUR LEADERS MAY LIVE
FULLY DEPENDENT ON YOU.

— VIGILANT CONCERN FOR THE GOVERNMENT —

It is impossible to have good government unless voters like you and those chosen for public office are governed by moral principles.

David Lawrence, former editor of *U.S. News and World Report*, put it well: "When people with a conscience choose governments with a conscience, then the promises men live by will be kept — and then only will conditions prevail that are conducive to peace in the world."

The blessings of liberty do not long stay in the hands of those who neglect them or take them for granted. God in His generosity showers us with countless benefits, but He always leaves us free to cherish or reject them.

Keep constantly in mind that your interest in government should be a never-ending job. The very nature of free government requires unremitting vigilance. It is much like maintaining the health of the body. It demands continuous attention and therefore continuing responsibility. Few permanent gains result from a hit-and-miss interest.

Whoever walks honestly walks securely.
Proverbs 10:9

KEEP ALL IN GOVERNMENT EVER CONSCIOUS OF
THEIR MORAL RESPONSIBILITY, O LORD.

– Little Sacrifices –

In 1808, Goethe made a comment that is as fresh and timely today as it was many years ago. Here are his words:

> To make large sacrifices in big things is what we are seldom capable of.

Most good people would die for their country, but too few will live for it. They could prevent wars by fulfilling faithfully and continually the numerous little details necessary for good health in politics and the administration of public affairs.

God expects us to have the good sense to see that success is the result of hard work and careful attention to the innumerable items that seem trifling but which are the stepping-stones to that success.

Remind as many as you can that there is something everyone can do to improve government. Many miss the forest for the trees by overlooking small duties that insure big success.

Show them the part that they can play in keeping politics clean and in getting many others to exercise their privilege of registering and voting.

Do not neglect to do good and to share
what you have; God is pleased by sacrifices of that kind.
Hebrews 13:16

O LORD, LET ME NEVER UNDERESTIMATE THE VALUE OF LITTLE ACTS
IN RAISING THE STANDARDS OF GOVERNMENT.

– It's Up to You –

James Madison, fourth President of the United States, believed in the people governing themselves. He said:

> We have staked the whole future of America not on the power of government, far from it, but on the capacity of mankind for self-government.

Almighty God put in the hands of every human being a bit of His power. He expects each individual not to keep it for himself alone but to apply it to the administration of human affairs.

The closer one is to God and the more one comprehends divine truth, the greater is his responsibility to bring into government that quality of truth and justice that is essential if right is to triumph.

What President Madison stressed many years ago is just as important today. No matter how perfect the form of government may be, little benefit comes from those high standards unless those who know the importance of self-government take the trouble to fulfill all the obligations which such a privilege requires.

Never forget that self-government will be a little stronger or weaker according to how you play your individual role.

> *Let every person be subordinate to the higher*
> *authorities, for there is no authority except*
> *from God, and those that exist have been*
> *established by God.*
> Romans 13:1

LET ME CONSCIENTIOUSLY PUT TO GOOD USE THE POWER YOU HAVE
PLACED IN MY HANDS, O HOLY SPIRIT.

— Victory in Defeat —

A young man, disturbed by lack of public interest in the running of government, felt that he, at least, should do his part. At considerable sacrifice, he ran for public office. But he lost the election.

He found consolation in his defeat, however, because he knew that his efforts had encouraged many citizens to take a more conscientious interest in political affairs. "I have no regrets," he wrote. "I proved my point and possibly made a small contribution toward better government."

Most people tend to forget that they can render an important service to the common good by suffering a loss themselves. In fact, it is often the most effective way to make a lasting contribution toward better government.

One who dares to undergo hardship, misunderstanding, and even defeat while working for the best interests of others is truly imitating the Redeemer. In his heart, he knows that he is winning for eternity even though losing from a worldly point of view.

*"What is impossible for human beings is
possible for God."*
Luke 18:27

Let me imitate you, O Savior, by seeking the divine gain of others even at a temporal loss to myself.

– GOOD WRITING –

Two young prisoners recently sawed their way to freedom through the bars of the Warwick, Virginia, jail. Later that same day they attended a movie about the Revolutionary War traitor Benedict Arnold.

After seeing the film, the fugitives meekly walked into police headquarters and surrendered. They said the picture made them "think." Conscience-stricken, they decided that the only right thing to do was to give themselves up.

A tremendous opportunity to spark the bit of good and greatness that is in every human being is within the grasp of movies, television, radio, books, magazines, as well as newspapers.

You can do much to improve the quality of the great channels of communications. But don't wait until you have something to complain about before speaking up.

It is far better to be positive and constructive. Encourage and praise writings and productions which reflect the God-given talent of those sincerely trying to discover the good in their fellow man rather than appeal to his lower nature.

When the intelligent hear a wise saying,
they praise it and add to it.
Sirach 21:15

BLESS, O LORD, ALL PRODUCERS, WRITERS, AND DIRECTORS,
WHO ARE TRYING TO BRING OUT THE BEST IN MAN.

– Where DeMille Got His Start –

Just after Cecil B. DeMille completed his picture *The Ten Com-mandments*, a reporter asked him how long it took to produce this extraordinary film. Mr. DeMille answered: "I am now seven-ty-five. I would say it took me seventy-five years."

His interest really started in his childhood when his father read aloud every night one chapter of the Old Testament and another from the New Testament.

When asked if he found time to read it nowadays, De Mille replied: "There are two Bibles on my night table which are a constant source of comfort and reference. My office has not been without a Bible since I first occupied it."

Also, asked why he placed so much value on the Bible, he said: "All men should value truth. Here is the source of truth. These truths are divinely inspired. It doesn't matter whether I believe this or don't believe it, or whether any other man does or doesn't. It is not a matter for opinion. Here, opinion is of no consequence. It is true, and this truth is unassailable by any mortal."

It is not by bread alone that people live,
but by all that comes forth from the mouth of the Lord.
Deuteronomy 8:3

Thanks to you, O my God, for your inspired word.

– Individuals Make a Union –

A trade unionist, who put up a valiant fight to raise the standards of his local, won a post on the executive board by a margin of 19 votes out of the 1,166 cast. He sent the following memorandum, based on Christopher principles, to his fellow members:

> Our union can never be any better than the individuals running it.
>
> Self-autonomy is impossible without self-participation. A good union starts with you. It will be as good as you and others like you make it.
>
> The results of the coming election will be of vital concern to every member.
>
> It is a human tendency to vote for self-interest rather than for the good of all concerned.
>
> Putting the welfare of our union above the interests of a particular party, group, or individual is one sure way to protect the democratic brotherhood to which we are all looking forward.
>
> Vote for those whom you know want to serve and will serve our union for the best interests of all.

No one should seek his own advantage,
but that of his neighbor.
1 Corinthians 10:24

BLESS, O LORD, THOSE WHO STRIVE TO STIR UP IN OTHERS
A SENSE OF PERSONAL RESPONSIBILITY.

– PEACE STARTS WITH YOU –

Have you ever read this ancient Chinese proverb about world peace? Here it is:

> If there is righteousness in the heart, there will be beauty in the character; if there is beauty in the character; there will be harmony in the home; if there is harmony in the home, there will be order in the nation; when there is order in the nation, there will be peace in the world.

Once enough people realize that the peace of the world starts with themselves, great headway will probably be made in achieving that precious blessing of peace for which most men yearn.

Jesus Christ came on earth to teach each of us how to live in peace here so that we could prepare for the endless happiness of heaven.

At the birth of Christ, the angels sang, "… on earth peace to those on whom his favor rests" (Luke 2:14). Thirty-three years later when He arose from the dead, His very first words were: "Peace be with you." And then He immediately added: "As the Father has sent me, so I send you" (John 20:21).

If you would be an apostle of peace, a peace-bearer or a Christ-bearer, fill your own heart with the peace of Christ and then share it with as many others as you can reach.

So love faithfulness and peace!
Zechariah 8:19

INSTILL IN ME A DEEP LOVE OF PEACE, O LORD.

– THE FIRST VOTE –

Some time ago Paul Antonio, a tinsmith, was hired to build and install the black steel ballot box now used by members of the United Nations Security Council at Lake Success when they cast their votes on world issues.

When the box was opened just before the first Security Council session, there was found at the bottom a brief message written in a clear handwriting on a cheap piece of notepaper. The message read:

> May I, who have had the privilege of constructing this ballot box, cast the first vote? May God be with every member of the United Nations Organization, and through your noble efforts bring lasting peace to us all — all over the world.
>
> (Signed) Paul Antonio, mechanic

By this one simple act did Antonio (a plain workman, like Joseph, the foster-father of Jesus) give the Council members a reminder of the importance of the supernatural. At the same time (because the incident was widely publicized for its human-interest angle) he got the same lesson over to millions in our land and throughout the world.

> *"Peace I leave with you; my peace I give to you.*
> *Not as the world gives do I give it to you."*
> John 14:27

LORD, OPEN ME TO EVERY OPPORTUNITY TO BRING TO OTHERS
THE TRUE MESSAGE OF PEACE.

— Your Right of Dissent —

Do you know the origin of the word "boycott"? If you look in the dictionary you will find that it came from Captain Boycott who was a land agent in Ireland in 1880. He acted so unreasonably toward his tenants that they felt their only protection was to form a league against him.

They knew that in justice they had a right to dissent, and so they individually agreed neither to rent from him nor to trade with him. Furthermore, they used every legitimate effort to keep others from doing so.

Before long, Captain Boycott saw that he had no choice but to live up to his obligations to those who rented or traded with him.

Ever since that time, the word "boycott" has signified the refusal of individuals or groups to do business with certain persons or to purchase specific products.

While it is important to avoid anything that is unfair or unjust when making a protest, nevertheless, one of the most effective ways to correct abuses is to take a courageous stand for what is just. Protect your right of dissent. Remember always that God has given you special powers as an individual. Don't underestimate the part that you can play.

Be firm, steadfast, always fully devoted to the
work of the Lord, knowing that in the Lord
your labor is not in vain.
1 Corinthians 15:58

HELP ME, O LORD, TO UPHOLD YOUR JUSTICE
AND STAND FOR WHAT IS RIGHT.

– How to Write an Effective Letter –

You can help shape public opinion if you take the trouble to write constructive letters to those in positions of influence. Here are a few tips:

1. *Be objective.* Stick to the truth and back up your opinions with facts. Exaggerations, emotional outbursts, or extremes of any kind detract from your point and often cause a letter to be dropped unread into the wastebasket.
2. *Think things through.* Instead of dashing off a few meaningless lines, take a few moments to clarify and coordinate your thought. This practice will add punch to your words.
3. *Write promptly; don't delay.* A brief note of praise or constructive criticism dispatched without delay makes a far greater impact than one sent when an issue is practically forgotten. Furthermore, postponement often means "never sent."

God wants you to show a personal responsibility toward the world in which you live. Letter writing can help you exert an influence for good.

> *"By your words you will be acquitted, and by your words you will be condemned."*
> Matthew 12:37

ALLOW ME, ALMIGHTY GOD, TO BE AN INSTRUMENT IN BRINGING YOUR LOVE AND TRUTH TO ALL MANKIND.

– Helping Others Helps Yourself –

Danny Carlsen, the founder of Narcotics Anonymous, was born in 1906. When he was sixteen, he developed a serious ear infection. To relieve the agonizing pain that resulted, his foster mother, a physician, gave him morphine tablets.

As a result, he became addicted to narcotics and remained so for the next twenty-five years. Nine of these years were spent behind prison bars. In 1949 he returned to New York City after his eighth stay in a hospital for addicts. He planned to lick the enemy with a new approach.

Twice a week he gathered together other addicts who wanted to throw off the shackles of the habit. By these meetings, and mutual encouragement based on the principles of Alcoholics Anonymous, many have been able again to start leading normal lives.

Danny's example shows us that one of the best ways to help ourselves is to help someone else. God's special aid is present when men intent on improving themselves make it their business to help others, too.

Bear one another's burdens, and so you will
fulfill the law of Christ.
Galatians 6:2

Lord, help me to help myself by helping others.

– A Successful Witness –

Like countless others, Albert Cox of Washington, D.C., found great inspiration in this prayer attributed to St. Francis of Assisi:

Lord, make me an instrument of Thy Peace! Where there is hatred, let me sow love; where there is injury, pardon; where there is doubt, faith; where there is despair, hope; where there is darkness, light; where there is sadness, joy!

O Divine Master, grant that I may not so much seek to be consoled, as to console; to be understood, as to understand; to be loved, as to love. For it is in giving that we receive; it is in pardoning that we are pardoned; and it is in dying that we are born to eternal life.

Mr. Cox had a longing to share with others his own source of inspiration. In true Christopher fashion he decided to do something about it. He sent it to *This Week* magazine. Even if they turned it down, at least he was trying, and God blesses those who try.

Much to his delight, not only did *This Week* print the prayer in its seven million copies, but the *Reader's Digest,* in its fifteen million copies, reprinted it with tribute to Mr. Cox. Bickford's Cafeterias in New York City distributed it to thousands of its customers. *This Week* said that of all the selections they had published, none brought as great a response as this simple prayer.

*"As for the seed that fell on rich soil, they are the ones who,
when they have heard the word, embrace it with a generous
and good heart, and bear fruit through perseverance."*
Luke 8:15

LORD, HELP ME TO SHARE WITH OTHERS THE JOYS
YOU HAVE GIVEN ME.

– F I V E –

Pray Always

Almost without exception, when I go through an airport I
have an interesting, spiritual encounter with someone. Do
people in airports want to talk about spiritual things because
they are fearful of travel? Or are they perhaps bored waiting for
flights and will talk to anyone who will listen? I'm not sure.

One evening while waiting for a delayed flight I sat down at
the airport bar to watch football and have a cold beer. It's funny
to see people's reactions when they see a priest come up to the
bar. Some want to hide, but most people are intrigued, and immediately begin conversation. Their guards are generally down
because they are on home turf, and I've come to them.

One especially interesting gentleman was thrilled I sat next
to him and made it very obvious that he was. I was a bit nervous
about his enthusiasm since I was hoping to watch in peace as my
team played the big game. After hearing the myriad of tragedies
that accompanied his fifty years of life, I couldn't help but be
impressed by his joyful and hopeful demeanor. We became fast
friends.

Dave told me that it was his faith in God that got him
through such tough times. Out of the blue I asked him how he
prayed. He responded immediately, "I've never prayed before."

"What do you mean?" I responded. "You said faith has got-
ten you through all of this."

"Yeah, I believe in God, but I don't know how to pray to
him."

I was shocked. Prayer to me has always been a natural consequence of faith. If I believe in God, I talk to him. But that's not

always the case. Like my new friend, Dave, many people imagine that prayer requires theological training.

As Father Keller understood so well, there is no formula for good prayer. Prayer is conversation with God. It is the turning of the human spirit toward its creator and Lord. Whether our conversation consists of praise, thanksgiving, petition, or even a simple groaning of soul, as long as we are directing our minds, hearts, or words to God, we are praying.

St. Paul exhorts us to "pray constantly." Is that even possible? Father Keller says yes, and he shows us how.

          ও

– Conversing with God –

Christ Himself gave us formal prayers, for example, the Our Father. But the type of prayer I propose can be as informal as one cares to make it. Absolute sincerity, naturally, is most important. And as you grow in this exercise of daily reflection and prayer — even though it be for no more than three minutes each day — you will find yourself talking to God with much the same ease as you would converse with a close friend. Use your own words in this simple, intimate chat with Our Lord, and they will gradually become your own personal, individual way of prayer.

You will find that the Holy Spirit is enlightening your mind and strengthening your will to do God's will as it is made known to you for the good of your own individual soul and for the good of others.

Regularity and continuity are most important. God's generosity will more than match your faithful effort. If you follow faithfully the practice of devoting at least three minutes a day to reflection and prayer, you will be happily surprised at the progress you will have made in the space of a few short months toward clarity of mind and *peace of soul*. Sinking your roots deep in the spiritual will help you to move from *passive* acceptance of truth to the *active* living of that truth as it bears upon the problems which beset you and the world.

The LORD is near to all who call upon him,
to all who call upon him in truth.
Psalm 145:18

LORD, MAY I ALWAYS SPEAK TO YOU AS SIMPLY AND DIRECTLY
AS I DO TO MY FRIENDS.

– Praying in God's Presence –

Before beginning your "three minutes a day" it would be well to stop and remind yourself that you are in the presence of God; that no matter who you are or what you are, God wants *you*, and is surrounding you now with His love and care. To you He says, as He said to St. Augustine: "You would not have sought Me had not I already been seeking you."

Such a brief moment of recollection of God's presence will enable your prayer to become the loving expression of loyalty on the part of a child for his father, a child who sees in his father not merely a provider of his needs but the one to whom he owes affection and devotion, because from him he has received life.

The Christopher who develops this practice of reflection and prayer, even in the elementary manner proposed here, will experience the growing reassurance that he or she does not work alone; that Christ works with and through each and every one who would be a Christopher. No matter what the difficulties or the degree of one's imperfections and inadequacies, he can help bring Christ into the marketplace of the world.

"Indeed he is not far from any one of us.
For 'In him we live and move and have our being.'"
Acts 17:27–28

LORD, I AM DELIGHTED THAT YOU ARE SEEKING ME AND THAT
I CAN CONVERSE WITH YOU IN YOUR HOLY PRESENCE.

– CHRIST BE WITH ME –

Fifteen hundred years ago St. Patrick composed his famous prayer, "The Breastplate," which has stirred the hearts of millions ever since.

Frequent reflection on even the small excerpt given here should be of immense value to each person who strives to bring Christ into the marketplace:

> Christ be with me, Christ in the front,
> Christ in the rear, Christ within me,
> Christ below me, Christ above me,
> Christ at my right hand, Christ at my left,
> Christ in the heart of every man who thinks of me,
> Christ in the mouth of every man who speaks to me,
> Christ in every eye that sees me,
> Christ in every ear that hears me,
> I bind unto myself the Name,
> The strong Name of the Trinity,
> By invocation of the same,
> The Three in One and One in Three.
> By Whom all nature hath creation,
> Eternal Father, Spirit, Word:
> Praise to the Lord of my salvation,
> Salvation is of Christ the Lord.

– Making Every Act a Prayer –

As I was sitting in the office of a busy college president one day, a little framed plaque with an interesting saying caught my eye. It was almost hidden behind a row of books, so as to be invisible to the casual visitor but constantly in the view of the man behind the desk.

Here are the words that this president made it a point to keep before him all through his day's work. The plaque read: *"Lord, I shall be verie busie this day. I may forget Thee, but do not Thou forget me."* These are the words of Sir Jacob Astley's memorable prayer before the battle of Newbury in the seventeenth century.

This simple thought suggests an important principle: by directing our "intention" we can make our every act a prayer. Thus our daily tasks are made more meaningful and more rewarding as well.

*And whatever you do, in word or in deed, do
everything in the name of the Lord Jesus,
giving thanks to God the Father through him.*
Colossians 3:17

Lord, help me to make my every act a prayer.

– MEAN WHAT YOU PRAY –

A recent magazine told the story of two little girls who were in danger of being late for school. "Let's stop and pray for God to get us there in time," one of them said.

"No," said the other, "let's run with all our might, and pray while we're running."

To pray effectively we must *mean* what we say. Obviously, the best way to show our intention is to make an effort in the right direction. If we are trying, God's help will not be absent. The supply of goodness is inexhaustible, always available, but we must show our own goodwill to put it into practice.

Do you not know that the runners in the
stadium all run in the race, but only one wins
the prize? Run so as to win.
1 Corinthians 9:24

LORD, I PRAY WITH ALL MY MIGHT;
HELP ME TO ACT ON WHAT I SAY.

– Praying in the Plural –

In praying, all of us should be especially careful to see that the words of our prayers do not become routine, that we do not pervert the meaning of the prayer for selfish personal ends.

A typical example of this kind of error is found when people pray, saying "Our Father" but meaning "*My* Father." Or saying "Give us this day" but meaning "Give *me* this day." Or "Forgive us our trespasses" replaced mentally by "Forgive *me*...." Christ did not accidentally make all the pronouns plural when He gave the prayer to His disciples as an example of how they should pray. Surely He meant for them to think of others as well as of themselves when they prayed. And the Christopher will always bear this in mind, knowing that he can do himself good only by working to better the lives of others. It is for them that he will especially pray.

We give thanks to God always for all of you,
remembering you in our prayers, unceasingly.
1 Thessalonians 1:2

Lord, teach me to pray for others,
not merely for myself.

– Are You Listening? –

His companions were making fun of the ragged barefoot boy. "You're a Christian," they taunted him. "If God really loves you, why doesn't He take better care of you? Why doesn't He tell someone to send you a pair of shoes?"

The boy seemed puzzled for a moment. Then, with tears in his eyes, he replied, "I think He does tell people. But they're not listening."

Those who strive to grow closer to Our Lord in prayer should find their minds and hearts growing larger each day. Their vision will take in more and more of life; their hearts will embrace more and more of their fellows.

Of course there is always the danger — one sees its effects too often — that those who strive to develop their inner lives will do so at the expense of consideration for their fellow men. To them the words of the Apostle John are most applicable:

This is the commandment we have from him: whoever loves God must also love his brother.
1 John 4:21

LORD, MAY I GROW IN LOVING YOU MORE, SO THAT I MIGHT PASS IT ON TO OTHERS.

— PRAY AND WORK —

An inexperienced boxer noticed that other contestants stopped for a short prayer just after entering the ring: He asked his trainer if it really did any good to pray before a boxing match.

"Yes, it does," the trainer said, "provided, of course, you know how to box."

God expects each of us to go through the painstaking effort of developing the natural talents He has given us, and not to expect Him to make up for our neglect.

Every quality of mind, heart, and soul that the Lord has entrusted to you is important in His divine plan. All of them have been given to you for a purpose much bigger than yourself. They should be cultivated and used for the temporal and eternal interests of others as well as your own.

Strive diligently to bring into play your natural ability, and you will fulfill the old axiom: "Pray as if everything depended on God, and work as if everything depended on yourself."

And we have this confidence in him, that if we
ask anything according to his will, he hears us.
1 John 5:14

IN DEPENDING ON YOU, O JESUS,
LET ME NOT FAIL TO DO MY PART.

– PRAY FOR THE GOVERNMENT –

All of us, at one time or another, may complain about our government. But how many of us actually *do* anything to make it better? In addition to our regular duties as citizens, we can give our government the very real benefit of our prayer. We can make up our own, or use the following Christopher prayer:

> Inspire us, O God, with such a deep love of our country that we will be actively concerned in its welfare as well as in that of all our fellow countrymen for time and for eternity. Teach us to show by word and deed the same zealous interest in protecting and furthering the Christian principles upon which our nation is founded that others display in belittling or eliminating them.
>
> Guide and strengthen the President, his Cabinet, the members of Congress, the delegates to the United Nations, the governor of our state, the officials of our community, and all others, in high position or low, who are entrusted with the task of protecting for all citizens those rights which come from You and from You alone.
>
> Teach us likewise to be worthy instruments in extending to all people of all nations, Your children and our brothers, the same peace, freedom, and security with which You have so abundantly blessed our land. Through Christ Our Lord. Amen.

– The Power of Intercession –

A Christopher prays for others, putting himself at the disposal of all. There are no exceptions. Not only can we pray for ourselves, for others whom we know — we can pray for the great majority in our country and over the world who have little or no knowledge of Christ. Even one minute a day of prayer would count for much.

One woman we know spends an hour each day in St. Patrick's Cathedral praying for the Secretary of State, that he may, in his official duties, uphold the Christian principles upon which this country was founded. All of us can follow her example, using this most powerful means to change the world for the better.

> *... and pray for one another, that you may be*
> *healed. The fervent prayer of a righteous*
> *person is very powerful.*
> James 5:16

LORD, I PRAY FOR ALL THE PEOPLE IN THE WORLD,
THAT THEY MAY COME TO KNOW AND LOVE YOU.

– GIVING THANKS –

When Cicero said: "Gratitude is not only the greatest of virtues, but the parent of all," he focused attention on a heavenly quality often overlooked in self-development.

Show others the appreciation and consideration that is due them, and you help yourself become a more complete person. Sincere gratitude is a sure way to hearten others who do not look for flattery, but who are understandably disappointed when even the ordinary courtesy of a simple "thank you" is overlooked.

Christ Himself was surprised when only one of the ten lepers He cured returned to thank Him. "Ten were cleansed, were they not? Where are the other nine? Has none but this foreigner returned to give thanks to God?" (Luke 17:17-18).

Do more than ask God for favors. Make every day a thanksgiving day by expressing your appreciation to God for creating you in His holy image and giving you an eternal destiny.

Show your gratitude to Him in a practical way by being as generous to others as He is to you.

THANKS TO YOU, O LORD OF LORDS,
FOR ALL THAT I AM AND HOPE TO BE.

– THE WONDER OF YOUR HEART –

"I cannot understand how any thinking person can deny there is a Supreme Being in back of all this creation." This thought dominated a letter sent to us by an eighty-two-year-old Ohio doctor.

"Take my heart, for instance," he continued. "It beats 72 times a minute — 4,320 times an hour — 108,680 times a day — 37,843,200 times a year — 3,103,142,400 times in 82 years, and still keeps beating day and night."

It is so easy for us to take for granted not only the constant beat of our hearts, but also the innumerable wonders of creation.

Pause from time to time and reflect prayerfully on them in the spirit of the Hebrew Psalmist, who joyfully proclaimed:

> *When I see your heavens, the work of your fingers,*
> *the moon and stars that you set in place —*
> *What is man that you are mindful of him,*
> *and a son of man that you care for him?*
> *Yet you have made him little less than a god,*
> *crowned him with glory and honor.*
> *You have given him rule over the works of your hands,*
> *put all things at his feet.*
> Psalm 8:4-7

MAY I SHOW BY MY WORDS AND DEEDS, O HOLY SPIRIT, THAT I TRULY REFLECT YOUR GLORY IN ALL THAT I SAY AND DO.

— A LIVING PRAYER —

Action should spring out of reflection and prayer. The mind *sees*: and with the help that God supplies, the will is moved to *do*. Your every effort at prayer deepens and strengthens your own spiritual power. As your spiritual power is deepened, you will desire more and more to bring something of that power to others. You must strive for self-sanctification. But you will go further than that, in the spirit of "love your neighbor as yourself" (Mark 12:31). You will want to bring the love of Christ to everyone — into the mainstream of life — *to reach the world with it as far as you can.*

If someone could follow us always and never let us forget the great fundamentals of life — the value of our individual soul, the deep love of God for each of us, the love we should have for all men as children of a common Father, and above all the eternity of either heaven or hell which will follow the end of our life here on earth — what changed beings we would be. We wouldn't make the mistakes we often make now through our failure to keep our minds fixed on these infallible truths. Instead, the life of each of us would be a living prayer which would affect not only ourselves but also the world.

In whatever you do, remember your last days,
and you will never sin.
Sirach 7:36

LORD, I GIVE YOU MY HEART AND MY MIND.
I SURRENDER TO YOU — GRANT THAT MY LIFE
MIGHT BE A LIVING PRAYER.

– S I X –

Becoming Like Christ

The ancient Greeks had it almost right. To their many gods they attributed exceptional human qualities. We call this "anthropomorphism," from the Greek word meaning "human form." Think of Aphrodite, the goddess of love, desire, and sexuality; Apollo, the god of music and the arts; Ares, the god of war and violence; Athena, the goddess of peace and intelligence; Hera, the goddess of marriage and family. And the list goes on and on of gods acting like superhuman people.

How is that "almost right"?

The Word became flesh
and made his dwelling among us. (John 1:14)

God became man. Or as St. Paul exclaimed, "We do not have a high priest who is unable to sympathize with our weaknesses, but one who has similarly been tested in every way, yet without sin" (Hebrews 4:15).

How amazing is that! While the Greeks imagined the divine as being superhuman, God, in fact, humbled himself, took on our form, so that we could become our best selves, made in his image and likeness. Not in their wildest dreams could the Greeks or anyone else, of any time or place, have imagined God becoming man to redeem us from our sins and elevate us to be like him.

In this chapter, Father Keller invites us on a journey of imitation of Christ. You will be inspired to renew your commitment to a virtuous life out of love for God. This is not a call to religiosity or moralistic living. Just the opposite. Father Keller's personal experience of God was the motor for everything he did. His desire to live virtuously was simply a desire to become more like his friend and brother Jesus. Like a younger brother who emulates his older brother, Father Keller saw the pursuit of the imitation of Jesus as a natural consequence of love for God.

As Father Keller now walks us through what living like Jesus looks like, get ready to fall in love with Jesus all over again, not in theory but in practice.

❧

– PERSEVERANCE BEARS FRUIT –

A young man, just beginning the study of musical composition, once went to Mozart to ask him the formula for developing the theme of a symphony. Mozart suggested that a symphony was rather an ambitious project for a beginner: perhaps the young man might better try his hand at something simpler first.

"But you were writing symphonies when you were my age," the student protested.

"Yes," the famous composer answered. "But I didn't have to ask how."

The beginner in any field is often impatient, eager for quick results. Yet the time spent in preparing a firm groundwork is not time wasted. Particularly is this true of those who would help others for the love of God. For most of us there is no quick, easy, or lazy way. It is a question of daily plodding, often in the face of discouragement, misunderstanding, and obstacles. Perseverance is the test of our sincerity.

We earnestly desire each of you to
demonstrate the same eagerness for the
fulfillment of hope until the end, so that you
may not become sluggish, but imitators of
those who, through faith and patience, are
inheriting the promises.
Hebrews 6:11-12

O HOLY SPIRIT, PRODUCE IN ME THE FRUIT OF PERSEVERANCE.

– An Oak or a Squash? –

A prominent businessman who was enrolling his son in a well-known university shook his head dubiously when he began to examine the institution's catalog of studies. "Does my son have to take all these courses?" he asked the dean. "Can't you make it shorter? He wants to get out quickly."

"Certainly he can take a shorter course," replied the dean. "But it all depends on what he wants to make of himself. When God wants to make an oak He takes twenty years, but He only takes two months to make a squash."

Shortcuts attract all of us. And of course we are free to take the easy way out. But just as oaks do not grow overnight, neither do the mind and character. We shall have to live for all eternity as we form ourselves here.

Long-suffering results in great wisdom;
a short temper raises folly high.
Proverbs 14:29

LORD, FORM IN ME THE VIRTUE OF PATIENCE SO THAT I
CAN BECOME THE BEST YOU INTEND FOR ME.

– A LITTLE BLACK BOOK –

A woman in California was the object of much curiosity in her neighborhood because of a most unusual habit. Every time she went into a store or a shop or a movie theater she would take a little black book out of her purse and write in it.

"Do you keep a record of everything you spend?" someone finally asked her.

"Oh no," she replied. "I only keep a list of what I buy in the way of luxuries ... perfumes, cigarettes, things like that."

"But what do you use the list for?" came back the query.

"Well, the fact is," this woman answered, "I feel so selfish enjoying my many comforts when there is so much suffering in the world. So I keep this list, and whenever I spend money for my own comfort, I give a like amount to charity for the homeless or the sick."

She had found her own way of looking at the world's misery. It is a good way, for the pain of one person is the pain of us all.

> *"In every way I have shown you that ... we*
> *must help the weak, and keep in mind the*
> *words of the Lord Jesus who himself said,*
> *'It is more blessed to give than to receive.' "*
> Acts 20:35

LORD, GRANT THAT I MAY BE PERSONALLY CONCERNED
TO HELP THOSE IN NEED.

– The Power of Encouragement –

"There is no surprise more magical than the surprise of being loved," Charles Morgan once said. "It is God's finger on man's shoulder."

There's a bit of nobility in the worst of human beings because all are made in God's image, and that image can never be completely effaced or lost. Even the man who has decided to have nothing whatsoever to do with God isn't frozen in that state of mind. Deep in the roots of his being — just because he is created in the Divine image — there is an ever-present tug toward his Maker.

It is the privilege of Christophers to help him become aware of this tremendous attraction. They can honestly say to anyone, with little danger of hurting his feelings: "There's a lot of good in you!" With a kind word or a friendly glance they can do much to inspire confidence. They never write anybody off!

No matter how desperate the case, no matter how ignoble the character, theirs is the unshakable conviction that there is always hope!

> *"This is how all will know that you are my*
> *disciples, if you have love for one another."*
> John 13:35

O LORD, HELP ME TO SEE YOUR IMAGE IN ALL PEOPLE AND
TO LOVE THEM, BECAUSE YOU MADE THEM FOR YOURSELF.

– Don't Just Feel Sorry, Do Something –

On a mountain trail in the Andes a traveler met a farmer riding on a mule, while his wife walked along behind him.

"Why isn't your wife riding?" the traveler asked the farmer.

"Because," the farmer replied, "she has no mule."

It is even possible, when you come to think of it, that the farmer felt sorry for his wife. He may have thought to himself, "Too bad my wife has to walk. Now if only she had a mule!"

How often we do this! How often we fail to help those in need, out of the abundance of the things we possess, yet feel sorry for them! We express sympathy and do nothing. And all the while there lie right at hand the means whereby we could relieve their burden.

"Then they will answer and say, 'Lord, when
did we see you hungry or thirsty or a
stranger or naked or ill or in prison, and not minister
to your needs?' He will answer them, 'Amen,
I say to you, what you did not do for one of
these least ones, you did not do for me.' "
Matthew 25:44-45

GRANT US, O LORD, TO KNOW NOT ONLY WHAT WE OUGHT TO DO,
BUT ALSO THE WAY IN WHICH WE CAN DO IT.

– Bearing Adversity –

Three hundred years ago a prisoner condemned to the Tower of London carved on the wall of his cell this sentiment to keep up his spirits during his long imprisonment:

It is not adversity that kills, but the impatience with which we bear adversity.

Rebelling against difficulties or obstacles that cannot legitimately be avoided only makes a bad situation worse. Ordinary common sense recommends that we ride the storm, not buck it. But going one step further — going from the natural to the supernatural — makes it easier still to bear adversity patiently.

Once you recognize that your suffering can actually bear fruit if you try to have the same purpose as Christ, then there will be the hidden joy of accomplishment even in bearing the cross which He bore for us two thousand years ago.

Accept whatever happens to you;
in periods of humiliation be patient.
For in fire gold is tested,
and the chosen, in the crucible of humiliation.
Sirach 2:4-5

O Lord, give me the grace to bear patiently
what must be borne for your sake.

– NO PAIN, NO GAIN –

Some years ago the late Dr. Alexis Carrel made an interesting statement about the need for self-discipline: "Everything has been made too easy for most of us," he said. "All life has aspired to the condition of ... minimum effort and maximum pleasure. Amusement has been the national cry; 'a good time' our chief concern. The perfect life as viewed by the average youth or adult is a round of ease or entertainment.... This indolent and undisciplined way of life has sapped our individual vigor, imperiled our democratic form of government.... Our race pitifully needs new supplies of discipline, morality, and intelligence."

Of course a *reasonable* share of pleasure is intended for each of us: God wants us to have it. But we must keep in mind that we are here only for a short time to prepare for eternity. Once secure in that knowledge, temperance will come much easier.

*"And when the last hour comes, you will begin
to think very differently of your whole past life;
and be exceedingly sorry that you have been
so negligent and reckless."*
Imitation of Christ (I:23, 20)

LORD, LET ME APPROACH THE DIFFICULT THINGS OF THIS LIFE
IN A WAY THAT LEADS TO PEACE IN THE LIFE TO COME.

– Recognizing Your Gifts –

A bricklayer whose brother happened to be a gifted and famous violinist once found himself in conversation with the head of the construction company for which he worked.

"It must be fine to have such a renowned man for a brother," the executive observed. And then, anxious not to offend his worker's pride, he continued: "Of course we must accept the fact that talent isn't evenly distributed — even in the same family."

"That's the truth," came back the reply. "Why, my brother doesn't know the first thing about bricklaying. It's a good thing he can afford to pay others to build his house for him."

It's not vanity to recognize our own place in life and our fitness for it. Instead of wasting our time envying others their talents, we should devote ourselves to the productive use of our own ability. God intends each of us for a special job, and He gives us the right tools.

> *"The one who had received two talents also came forward and said, 'Master, you gave me two talents. See, I have made two more.' His master said to him, 'Well done, my good and faithful servant. Since you were faithful in small matters, I will give you great responsibilities. Come, share your master's joy.' "*
> Matthew 25:22-23

LORD, HELP ME TO RECOGNIZE THE TALENTS YOU HAVE GIVEN ME, AND TO PUT THEM TO WORK FOR YOU.

− RULING OURSELVES −

Frederick the Great of Prussia was walking along a road on the outskirts of Berlin one day when accidentally he brushed against a very old man. "Who are you?" Frederick asked out of idle curiosity as the two came to a halt.

"I am a king," the old man answered.

"A king?" echoed Frederick. "Over what principality do you reign?"

"Over myself," was the proud reply. "I rule myself because I control myself. I am my own subject to command."

All of us can be kings, in the sense of the old man's words. But how many of us actually are? Instead of being in command, often we let ourselves be ruled over by the tyrants of temper or laziness or passion. We cannot hope to influence others if we are, as the common expression puts it, "not ourselves." And we can only be ourselves by controlling ourselves.

Therefore, sin must not reign over your mortal
bodies so that you obey their desires.
Romans 6:12

LORD, HELP ME TO RULE OVER MY PASSIONS
SO THAT YOU MAY RULE OVER ME.

– Your Turn at Bat –

A gentleman walking along the street passed a vacant lot where some boys were playing baseball. He asked one of the youngsters what the score was.

"We're behind, eighteen to nothing" was the answer.

"Well," said the gentleman, "I must say you don't look very discouraged."

"Discouraged?" the boy said, puzzled, "We're not discouraged. We haven't come to bat yet!"

There is a thought in this little anecdote that could cheer us all: on those days when life seems to be defeating us, when small trials come in a series, we can then think of life as a kind of baseball game, and patiently wait our turn at bat. Moreover, we can have the confidence of a winning team, since we have a Captain incapable of failure.

In all these things we conquer overwhelmingly
through him who loved us.
Romans 8:37

Lord God, please give me the confidence
that comes from trusting you.

– Antidotes for Being Judgmental –

An anonymous author has given expression to a valuable thought which calls for no comment from us:

- "When the other fellow acts that way, he's *ugly*. When you do it, it's *nerves*.
- "When he's set in his ways, he's *obstinate*. When you are, it's just *firmness*.
- "When he doesn't like your friends, he's *prejudiced*. When you don't like his, you are simply *showing good judgment of human nature*.
- "When he tries to be accommodating, he's *polishing the apple*. When you do it, you're using *tact*.
- "When he takes time to do things, he is *dead slow*. When you take ages, you are *deliberate*.
- "When he nitpicks, he's *cranky*. When you do, you're *discriminating*."

> *"For as you judge, so will you be judged,*
> *and the measure with which you measure will be*
> *measured out to you."*
> Matthew 7:2

LORD, HELP ME TO SEE MY OWN FAULTS AND
FORBEAR THE FAULTS IN OTHERS.

– SELFLESS SERVICE –

In the Revolutionary War, during preparations for a battle, a man in civilian clothes passed a corporal who was arrogantly ordering his men to lift a heavy beam. The man stopped and asked the corporal, "Why don't you help them."

"Sir," the answer came back indignantly. "I am a corporal!"

With a muttered apology, the stranger stripped off his coat and pitched in to help the soldiers.

"Mr. Corporal," he said, when the task was done, "whenever you haven't enough men to do a job, call on your commander in chief. I'll be glad to help."

With that, George Washington put on his coat and left.

To help others we must often humble ourselves; but, paradoxically enough, we always win by doing so. The best proof of this is Christ himself. He became the friend and servant of the lowest among men, lepers and beggars and thieves. And for this all mankind reveres Him.

"The greatest among you must be your servant."
Matthew 23:11

LORD, WITH ALL MY HEART I WANT TO SERVE YOU
BY SERVING OTHERS.

— OVERCOMING FAILURE —

One example that can serve as a model for all of how a man in public service actually built his life and accomplishments upon defeats is that of Abraham Lincoln.

The following, mostly failures, punctuated his life:

1. Lost job 1832
2. Defeated for legislature 1832
3. Failed in business 1833
4. Elected to legislature 1834
5. Sweetheart died 1835
6. Had nervous breakdown 1836
7. Defeated for Speaker 1838
8. Defeated for nomination for Congress 1843
9. Elected to Congress 1846
10. Lost re-nomination 1848
11. Rejected for land officer 1849
12. Defeated for U.S. Senate 1854
13. Defeated for nomination for Vice President 1856
14. Again defeated for Senate 1858
15. Elected President 1860

You, too, in God's Providence, can, despite all obstacles, do great things for your country — for your world!

I am convinced that neither death, nor life, nor angels, nor principalities, nor present things, nor future things, nor powers, nor height, nor depth, nor any other creature will be able to separate us from the love of God in Christ Jesus our Lord.
Romans 8:38-39

LET ME LEARN THROUGH IMITATION OF YOUR SUFFERING,
O CRUCIFIED SAVIOR, HOW TO SERVE OTHERS.

– Making the Right Choice –

Medical tests show that drugs can slow down or speed up a person's faculties but cannot bring about a better way of thinking.

People who believe drugs can cure nervousness, one medical authority said, will be disappointed. This doctor said:

> Drugs sometimes, wisely used, can help a person, but unless you want to help yourself, by learning not to let every "little family friction" get the better of you, there's no use in trying drugs. Remember, all of us have these "little frictions," but we learn to ignore them, or meet them calmly....

No matter how much people may try to avoid it, there is no substitute for each and every individual thinking and acting for himself. God meant it that way. He intended that one and all without exception should exercise the intelligence and free will needed to be master of his own destiny.

Heaven is generous with its help and graces, but all of this is provided more or less as man cooperates by showing the needed initiative on his own part.

What I do, I do not understand. For I do not
do what I want, but I do what I hate.
Romans 7:15

LET ME DISPLAY AT ALL TIMES, O LORD, THE SELF-CONTROL
OF MY HEART, MIND, SOUL, AND BODY THAT YOU EXPECT
OF A RESPONSIBLE PERSON.

– SPIRITUAL GROWTH –

Once I watched some children plant seeds in a garden. I saw the careful attention with which they watered them. Then the next morning the children rushed to the window, expecting to see the garden filled with blooms. In their disappointment and impatience they proceeded to neglect the garden and finally the seeds died without ever having produced anything.

This simple experience can be an example to all Christophers not to be impatient of results. The true bearer of Christ does not expect his good work to bear immediate fruit. He does not expect to plant a seed and get a rosebush overnight. Indeed, he may labor at length and apparently in vain. But the truth is that he is winning all the time, because it is the labor itself that counts. As Paul said:

> *I planted, Apollos watered, but God caused the*
> *growth. Therefore, neither the one who plants*
> *nor the one who waters is anything, but only*
> *God, who causes the growth.*
> 1 Corinthians 3:6-7

LORD, HELP ME TO COMBINE IN MYSELF GOODWILL, COURAGE, AND PATIENCE.

– Laying Down Your Life –

A doctor tells this story of an eight-year-old boy whose sister was dying of a disease from which the boy himself had recovered some time before. Realizing that only a transfusion of her brother's blood would save the little girl, the doctor asked the boy: "Would you like to give your blood for your sister?"

The child hesitated for a moment, his eyes wide with fear. Then, finally, he said: "Sure, Doctor, I'll do it."

Only later, after the transfusion was completed, did the boy ask hesitantly, "Say, Doctor, when do I die?"

Then the doctor understood the momentary hesitation and fear. It had taken the boy that long to decide to sacrifice his life for his sister.

Heroic bravery isn't limited only to grown-ups or to soldiers or firemen. It takes real courage to face sacrifice, to be willing to give ourselves up for others.

The way we came to know love was that he
laid down his life for us; so we ought to lay
down our lives for our brothers.
1 John 3:16

Lord, please give me the grace to
lay down my life for my friends.

Living as a Christian

My all-time favorite parable is "The Prodigal Son," or per-haps more aptly named, "The Parable of the Two Sons." If we wonder what God thinks of us, especially when we have sinned and feel unworthy of his love and mercy, we don't need to go any further than Luke 15:11-32. We all know the story. The younger son boldly requests of his father his portion of the inheritance, even before his father's death, so that he can enjoy it while he is still young. The father grants his son's wish, and the son goes off into a foreign land and wastes his money on loose living. When a famine takes over the land, he finds himself broke and hungry. He eventually comes to his senses and goes back to his father's house to ask for forgiveness and beg the father to al-low him to work in his home as just another servant. The father sees the son coming from a distance and goes out to meet him, embracing him, and bringing him back into the family with a huge celebration. Who doesn't love to hear Jesus describe for us that kind of divine love!

But believe it or not, there's another part of the parable that makes it my favorite. It's the conversation between the disgrun-tled older son and his father. The son is beside himself that his younger, wayward brother, who has caused so much trouble in the family, would be back in the fold with no consequences. Jesus goes to great length to show how resentful and angry the older son had become. The Lord says that the older son even refuses to enter into the house where the welcome home party is in full swing. Jesus tells us that the older son says to his father, "All these years I have served you [other translations say "slaved for you"] and not once did I disobey your orders; yet you never gave me even a young goat to feast on with my friends." The father's response gets to the heart of his son's issue, an issue of identity. While the son considered himself perfect because he had slaved for his father without any disobedience, the father saw him not as a servant or a slave but as his son, an equal partner of all that he had. "My son, you are here with me always; everything I have is yours" (Luke 15:31).

How do you see your relationship with God? The biggest stealer of our joy is not sin itself, but rather attachment to sin. The older brother was attached to his pride. He couldn't experience his father's love and generosity because his world revolved around himself.

So who is God for you? Is God a "cop" you try to avoid? Is he a vending machine that you go to when you need a favor? Father Keller doesn't think that this kind of relationship with God will make for a fulfilling life, mostly because like the father in the parable of the two sons, all that is God's is already ours. He wants to share that with us. He wants to gift us with blessings beyond our imagination.

In this next chapter, Father Keller continues to walk us through how to respond to God's grace in our lives. In his eminently practical style, he encourages us to live the adventure of the Christian life, united with our loving Father, in every area of our busy lives.

∾

– LIVING IN GOD'S PRESENCE –

Every sound made by a young couple and their three children during a two-week test was recorded on thirty-eight miles of electronic tape — unknown to them!

During the scientific test of survival techniques at Princeton University, they were confined to an 8' by 9' by 8' "fallout" shelter.

When hearing of the hidden microphone, the mother of the family was a bit embarrassed and said, "Of course we would have lived differently if we had known we were being recorded."

All of us would live differently if we realized that each of our thoughts, words, and deeds was on a record kept by God Himself.

Never forget the astounding fact that you are always in the presence of God, Who loves you dearly.

This conviction can stimulate you to look for opportunities of sharing that love with others as far as you can reach. You need never worry about having your record heard or seen if you do.

I observe your precepts and testimonies;
all my ways are before you.
Psalm 119:168

LET ALL MY ACTIONS, O LORD, REFLECT YOUR LOVE AND GOODNESS,
AND MAY THEY BE A CREDIT TO YOU.

– Where Do You Want to Go? –

In an English churchyard the following epitaph is carved on one of the ancient headstones:

> Remember, man that passeth by,
> As thou art now, so once was I.
> And as I am so thou must be;
> Prepare thyself to follow me.

Some visitor with a sense of discrimination scribbled the following underneath:

> To follow thee's not my intent,
> — Unless I know which way thou went.

It's easy to wander through life aimlessly, seldom giving any thought to the fact that the ultimate destination for each of us is either heaven or hell.

Where each of us goes depends on where he *wants to go.*

On what we do, or fail to do, over a lifetime for the love of God and others, as well as for ourselves, depends our eternal destination.

"But the one who perseveres to the end will be saved."
Matthew 24:13

LORD, I WANT TO BE WITH YOU FOREVER IN HEAVEN;
HELP ME TO FIX MY MIND AND HEART ON THIS GOAL.

– It's God's Idea –

The English novelist H. G. Wells once called upon the American novelist Henry James. In the drawing room of James's house Wells noticed a large and peculiar stuffed bird.

"My dear James," he said, astonished, "what is that?"

"That," James replied, "is a stork."

"Humph," Wells snorted. "It's not my idea of a stork."

"Apparently, however," came the answer, "it was God's idea of one."

Frequently our idea of something may not be God's idea; subconsciously, we may even feel that *our* idea is better. But the Creator's plan is above our logic. When we accept it, we find ourselves quickly in tune with life, more able to act constructively, to create according to the will of God, instead of blundering along in our private confusion.

> *Straight are the paths of the LORD,*
> *the just walk in them.*
> Hosea 14:10

GIVE US, O LORD, THE WISDOM TO SEE YOUR WAYS,
AND THE COURAGE TO WALK THEREIN.

– Eternity Now –

A plant fossil discovered in the San Juan Mountains of Colorado is believed to be 165 million years old. This would make it the oldest known specimen of a flowering plant. The palm-like growth left its imprint on red rock — the largest, 18 inches long. Fossil experts found 7 imprints — all of which are at least 10 million years older than the fossil of a flowering plant found in Normandy and previously said to be the oldest.

It is difficult for any of us to think in terms of a thousand years, much less a million. And yet, what is even a million years compared to eternity!

Scientists point out that the universe is 13.8 billion years old. These are staggering figures and should make us pause and reflect on the fact that each of us has already begun an eternity that will never end no matter how many billions of years pass.

Almighty God created each of us in His own sacred image. He offers us an eternity of supreme happiness with Him. But He leaves us free to take it or reject it.

Contemplate frequently on the tremendous implications of what Christ meant when He said:

> *"Come, you who are blessed by my Father.*
> *Inherit the kingdom prepared for you from the*
> *foundation of the world."*
> Matthew 25:34

HELP ME, O LORD, TO LIVE WELL THIS LIFE THAT WILL NEVER END.

– BUILDING ON ROCK –

Over and over again Christ stresses that we must be "doers," not "hearers" only. Vague intentions are not enough. We must use the inspiration of Christ's words as our point of departure. But we must translate them into action, not merely build spiritual castles in the air. Our house will be built upon a rock in proportion as each of us not only *hears* but actually *does* what Christ tells us.

> *"Everyone who listens to these words of mine*
> *and acts on them will be like a wise man who*
> *built his house on rock. The rain fell, the*
> *floods came, and the winds blew and buffeted*
> *the house. But it did not collapse; it had been*
> *set solidly on rock. And everyone who listens*
> *to these words of mine but does not act on*
> *them will be like a fool who built his house*
> *on sand. The rain fell, the floods came, and the*
> *winds blew and buffeted the house. And it*
> *collapsed and was completely ruined."*
> Matthew 7:24-27

GRANT ME, O LORD, BOTH TO HEAR AND TO DO YOUR WILL.

– Study for Life –

A high-school girl, seated next to a famous astronomer at a dinner party, struck up a conversation with him by asking: "What do you do for a living?"

"I study astronomy," he replied.

"Really?" said the teenager, wide-eyed. "I finished astronomy last year."

Many people stop growing mentally and spiritually at an early age. Physically, they continue to develop, but spiritually they remain as six-year-olds. Yet most of us — like the famous English writer and teacher who had the habit of listing his occupation always as "student" — do recognize that we have a lot to learn, especially in those things which concern us spiritually.

The words and actions of other people are one of the best sources of learning. By appreciating those around us, by realizing how much one can share with them and gain from them, we inevitably grow daily in knowledge and in love.

Wisdom cries aloud in the street,
in the open squares she raises her voice.
Proverbs 1:20

O Lord, help me to grow each day in knowledge
and love of others.

– BE ON GUARD –

In any well-disciplined army particular attention is given to the system of sentinels and guards. Any stranger approaching camp is challenged and made to identify himself. This is the case not only near the front line, but even in base areas distant from any actual fighting.

To the unthinking soldier such insistence might seem foolish, but in actuality it is just the opposite. A good soldier, engaged in a life-and-death struggle, must develop the *habit* of wariness; he must learn always to be on the watch for the enemy.

Many of us think of evil as something obvious, wearing a big label and hence easily avoided. But the forces of evil are a clever enemy, full of disguises, ready at all times to penetrate our defenses if we once relax. The true bearer of Christ is always on the alert, his eye and ear prepared to catch the first sign of the enemy's advance.

*"Be vigilant at all times and pray that you
have the strength to escape the tribulations
that are imminent."*
Luke 21:36

GUARD MY MIND AND HEART, LORD, THAT I MIGHT STAY
ALERT TO THE DANGERS OF EVIL.

– No Man Is an Island –

It's hard for any of us to realize that any time another suffers, we also are affected. But if we are true to our Christian belief, this is exactly the case. As John Donne, the famous poet, wrote several hundred years ago:

> The Church is Catholic, universal; so are all her actions. All that she does belongs to all. When she baptizes a child, that action concerns me.... All mankind is of one Author.... No man is an island, entire of itself. Every man is a piece of the continent, a part of the main. If a clod be washed away by the sea, Europe is the less.... Any man's death diminishes me, because I am involved in mankind.

Many people today have a "leave-me-alone" point of view; they don't want to "get involved" in anything. But the fact of the matter is that they are, as Donne says, "involved in mankind." When they realize this and act in harmony with their fellow men, they begin to live more fully.

We, though many, are one body in Christ and
individually parts of one another.
Romans 12:5

THANK YOU, LORD, FOR BRINGING ME INTO THE BODY OF CHRIST.
MAY I FIND MY GIFTS AND USE THEM IN SERVICE
OF THE CHURCH AND THE WORLD.

– PLAYING OUR PART –

William L. Stidger, in the magazine *Your Life*, tells a story about the conductor Walter Damrosch, who once stopped his orchestra when everything was apparently going along smoothly, and asked: "Where is the seventh flute? Where is the seventh flute?"

As Mr. Stidger points out, the conductor didn't ask for the first flute, or the second — but the seventh. Even the seventh flute had an important place in creating the harmony the leader desired.

"We may feel inferior, untalented, not even beautiful, and some of us uneducated," Mr. Stidger comments, "but each of us has a part to play and should play it well."

He tells how he used to watch the man who plays the triangle in a large orchestra. Often the player would sit through the entire number, eagerly waiting. Then, toward the close, he would, with perfect timing, deftly touch the instrument and produce just the right note.

In other words, there is no really unimportant job. We should do well whatever it is our part to do.

Now you are Christ's body, and individually
parts of it.
1 Corinthians 12:27

LORD, GIVE ME THE WISDOM AND GRACE TO USE
MY GIFTS TO DRAW OTHERS TO YOU.

– The Anchor of Hope –

Down through the centuries the anchor has been known as a symbol of safety. Taking a firm grip on the ocean floor, it can keep a ship from being swept aground in stormy weather.

Early Christians saw another symbol in the anchor — that of hope. In the catacombs and in early Christian art, the anchor was repeatedly used as a constant reminder of hope in Christ as the Way to salvation. It served also as a symbol of the cross of Christ that all must be willing to bear if they would be true followers of Him.

St. Paul, in writing to the Hebrews, recommended that all who would lead a truly spiritual life should have hope. "As an anchor of the soul, sure and firm" (Hebrews 6:19).

In the midst of the many trials and tribulations that the average person must face sooner or later in life, there is often a tendency to become cynical and pessimistic, if one lacks the faith, hope, and charity that can come from God alone.

The more you anchor your whole heart, mind, and soul in the love of Jesus Christ, the better you will be able to withstand the storms of life and help others to do the same.

For in hope we were saved.
Romans 8:24

In all that I think, say, and do, O Lord,
let me place my entire hope in you.

— THANKFULNESS —

A few days after Christmas a six-year-old boy was trudging down San Francisco's crowded Pine Street, dragging a glistening new wagon with a tiny baby passenger. The passenger was the statue of the Christ Child from the crib of the neighborhood church. Horrified, the boy's mother ran down the street and reprimanded her son sharply.

"But, Mother," the boy protested, wide-eyed, "I promised the Baby Jesus that if He gave me a wagon for Christmas, He would have the first ride in it."

But for us, every day is a most appropriate time to express our thanks to God for the blessings He has showered on all of us. Show Him your appreciation in any manner you wish — but *do* show Him. One way would be to reach beyond your own little circle into the big world, doing your part to bring the love of Christ into the marketplace.

> *Be filled with the Spirit, … giving thanks*
> *always and for everything in the name of our*
> *Lord Jesus Christ to God the Father.*
> Ephesians 5:18, 20

I GIVE YOU THANKS, O LORD, FOR ALL YOUR GOODNESS TO ME.
MAY I HAVE THE GRACE TO DO GOOD TO OTHERS.

– Real Joy –

"Sorrow is brief, but joy is endless" was the discerning comment of Johann Schiller, the German poet who died in 1805.

Man is forever seeking joy that is real and lasting. But he usually expects to possess it through physical self-gratification.

Although there are many alluring worldly pleasures, care must be taken not to confuse these with the true joy which has its roots in the deep recesses of the heart, mind, and soul.

The craving for material pleasure is never completely satisfied. Its fruits vanish all too quickly for those pursuing them. And all too often the price for indulgence is a high and demanding one.

Joy, on the other hand, is a gift directly from heaven. It can be enjoyed by both poor and rich, young and old, free and oppressed. It carries no cost beyond that of a good conscience and an abiding sense that the best earth can offer is a poor substitute for what the Lord promises those who love Him through thick and thin.

"You will grieve, but your grief will become joy."
John 16:20

KEEP ME AWARE, O HOLY SPIRIT, OF THE DIFFERENCE
BETWEEN LASTING JOY AND PASSING PLEASURE.

– WE ARE NOT ALONE –

One day, as fiction has it, the Devil decided to go out of business. His tools, therefore, being for sale, were put on display; and Malice, Jealousy, and Pride were soon recognized by most of his prospective customers. There was one worn, tiny, wedge-shaped tool bearing the highest price, however, which seemed difficult to identify.

"What is that?" someone asked. "I can't quite place it."

"Oh that!" Satan answered. "That is Discouragement. It is my most valuable tool. With it I can open many hearts, since so few people know that it belongs to me."

One of the most effective protections against discouragement is the comforting conviction that, as a Christopher, or Christ-bearer, we do not work alone. Christ is ever with us. We are His instruments, no matter how defective we may be.

"And behold, I am with you always, until the end of the age."
Matthew 28:20

COME, LORD JESUS, AND STRENGTHEN ME FOR MY SERVICE.

– Winning Through Suffering –

The seeming defeat of Good Friday must have been a tragic blow for the handful of apostles and disciples of the crucified Master.

Devoted as they were to Him, they were still the victims of their own human weakness. The temptation to lose heart after their Divine Leader had been executed must have tormented their natural inclination to think in terms of worldly rather than divine values.

If you would play a role in the sanctification of a world that either does not know or disdains divine love and truth, you must be ready to go through similar trials and temptations.

Seen through human eyes, your best efforts may often seem doomed to defeat and failure. But it is in the midst of such discouraging circumstances that you may be truly winning in a divine sense.

Often look at the cross of Christ and reflect on the fact that you, too, must appear to lose in this world in order to gain for eternity.

"Whoever seeks to preserve his life will lose it,
but whoever loses it will save it."
Luke 17:33

GRANT, O LORD, THAT I MAY ALWAYS ENDURE MY TRIALS
AND PUT COMPLETE TRUST IN YOU.

– A Healthy Optimism –

As William Dean Howells and Mark Twain were coming out of church one morning it commenced to rain heavily.

"Do you think it will ever stop?" asked Howells.

"It always has," answered Twain.

Unpleasant situations have a way of appearing eternal, but we can always bear in mind that nothing in this world is permanent. There is no evil that we cannot attack by faith, by good works, and by our prayers.

In this sense, a "healthy optimism" seems the natural point of view for all true believers in Christ's goodness.

Rejoice in the Lord always. I shall say it again: rejoice!
Philippians 4:4

Lord, I rejoice in you, especially when I face challenges and problems.

– TRUE HUMILITY –

Paul Cézanne never knew that he was later to be considered "the father of modern painting." Because of his great love for his work, he never thought of recognition. He struggled for thirty-five years, living in oblivion at Aix, giving away masterpieces to indifferent neighbors.

And then one day a discerning Paris dealer happened upon his canvases and, gathering several of them, presented the first Cézanne exhibit. The great of the art world were stunned: here, indeed, was a master!

And Cézanne himself was no less astonished. Arriving at the gallery on the arm of his son, he gazed wonderingly at his paintings, and tears came to his eyes.

"Look," he whispered. "They've framed them!"

Had it been Cézanne's chief aim to be hailed as a great artist, he might never have achieved much of anything. But he did achieve *greatness* simply by trying to make use of the artistic talents God had given him, in the very best way he knew how.

*... Or am I seeking to please people? If I were
still trying to please people, I would not be
a slave of Christ.*
Galatians 1:10

LORD, I WANT TO PLEASE YOU WITH
EVERYTHING I SAY AND DO.

– ANTIDOTE FOR PRIDE –

A device the Devil uses with great success when he wishes to cripple a worthy project is the stirring up of petty pride among those concerned. This is an evil which, by infecting even one or two, can nip in the bud the most promising enterprise for good.

And, with typical deception, this type of deadly pride, which aims at tripping up high-minded persons and ruining much good that could be done, persists in the name of virtue. As the poet Coleridge well said:

And the Devil did grin, for his darling sin
Is pride that apes humility.

Since this treacherous vice so often appears in harmless garb and manifests itself in so many disguises, we should be especially alert to see that we do not succumb to it ourselves.

We can better avoid the pitfalls of pride by concentrating our minds and hearts on the practice of *true* humility which is rooted in the knowledge that all we are and all we have comes from God.

"Without me you can do nothing."
John 15:5

I SURRENDER MY LIFE TO YOU, LORD, AND I RELY ON YOU
FOR EVERYTHING.

– MAKING NO EXCUSES –

A young boy who had shot and killed four children was asked why he did it. "I always wondered what it would be like to kill somebody," came the reply.

The examining board to which he was sent before trial decided he was "possessed of a mental condition which could affect his criminal responsibility." But one of the board members, in a dissenting opinion, stated that the boy was still *personally responsible* for his crime.

There is today an increasingly dangerous tendency to evade the facts — to place all the blame for all sin on anything and everything *except one's own personal choice*, one's own free, responsible act of will.

When a person continually offers evasive excuses for his own misdeeds, he eventually becomes entangled in his own rationalizations. It is much more practical to be honest about the situation and face the facts. And to do this will help eliminate additional trouble in the future.

If we say, "We are without sin" we deceive
ourselves, and the truth is not in us.
1 John 1:8

LORD, GIVE ME AN HONEST WILLINGNESS TO TAKE THE
CONSEQUENCES OF MY DELIBERATE DECISIONS.

— HABIT FORMING —

We've all had this happen to us: Try to break a piece of rope and find it too strong for us. Then the only thing to do is unravel the rope and break it strand by strand — a difficult and sometimes impossible procedure.

It's the same way with habits. For example, few of us indulge in really great deceits, but for some of us hardly a day goes by without our telling an "innocent" lie or committing some "harmless" act of dishonesty. But these insignificant sins build up a kind of tolerance in us, and soon we find our sense of right and wrong less sharp.

Good habits work the same way in reverse. If we get in the habit of goodness, of performing small acts of kindness and generosity, we soon discover that goodness comes easy to us: in big things as well as small.

A three-ply cord is not easily broken.
Ecclesiastes 4:12

HELP ME, O LORD, TO SNAP THE FIRST THREAD OF A BAD HABIT
BEFORE IT IS SPUN INTO AN UNBREAKABLE CABLE.

– Hold Your Tongue –

Someone once said that "thoughtless, catty remarks about others have probably created more unnecessary enemies than any other form of human relationship."

A Christopher above all others should take particular pains to see that his tongue is used for good, never for evil; to console, not to condemn; to build up, not to tear down; to rejoice at the good fortune of others, never to begrudge them success.

Though seldom admitted, gossip is one of the most dangerous of sins. Sometimes it may amount to nothing more than a seemingly harmless word, maybe nothing more than a slight inflection, yet the effect is often deadly — and permanent. A reputation can easily be damaged or even killed in a matter of moments. And without a chance for one word of defense on the part of the person misrepresented.

Even if the fault of another is true — and known — gossip about it serves no useful purpose and is sinful. To offer a charitable word of mercy, of excuse, of forgiveness is the Christlike approach.

The tongue is a small member and yet has
great pretensions. Consider how small a fire
can set a huge forest ablaze.
The tongue is also a fire.
James 3:5-6

Teach me, O Lord, to encourage the good in others,
not to be a faultfinder.

— Bearing Good Fruit —

A reporter called on Thomas A. Edison one afternoon to interview him about a substitute for lead in the manufacture of storage batteries that the scientist was seeking. Edison informed the man he had made twenty thousand experiments, but none of them had worked.

"But aren't you discouraged by all this waste of effort?" the reporter asked, amazed.

"Waste!" exclaimed Mr. Edison, "There's nothing wasted. I have discovered twenty thousand things that won't work."

From time to time we may feel that some good action of ours has not borne fruit. But we should not be discouraged: easy success is more likely to harm us than gradual achievement. And often an action that may seem in vain can have a delayed, important effect, like a seed ripening into grain.

Every spiritual act directed toward God is guaranteed its effect as far as our own spiritual welfare is concerned.

"But the seed sown on rich soil is the one who
hears the word and understands it, who indeed
bears fruit and yields a hundred or sixty or thirtyfold."
Matthew 13:23

LORD, LEAD ME TO ACTS OF LOVE THAT WILL BEAR GOOD FRUIT.

– LITTLE THINGS MEAN A LOT –

"Little and often make much in the end," runs an old German proverb.

Too few realize that little thoughts, prayers, words, and deeds can be stepping stones to greatness.

We of the Christophers keep repeating that it is "better to light one candle than to curse the darkness" — that doing something constructive, however small, can help solve big problems.

Christ Himself reminds us of the eternal worth of tiny deeds. He singled out the "poor widow" who gave "two mites" and promised an eternal reward to anyone who gave "a cup of cold water" to one of His "little ones."

The gentle Master also said that failure to give food, drink, or clothing to "one of the least ones," to refuse to take in a stranger, or to visit a person sick or in prison would merit "everlasting punishment."

Remember that the slightest efforts are part and parcel of His divine plan.

"The person who is trustworthy in very small matters is also trustworthy in great ones."
Luke 16:10

KEEP ME MINDFUL, O LORD, THAT WHAT I DO DOES
MAKE A DIFFERENCE IN THIS WORLD.

– KEEP JUMPING –

"May I ask you the secret of success?" an ambitious young man said to a successful merchant.

"There is no easy or simple secret," the merchant answered. "You must be on the alert for little things and jump at opportunities."

"But how can I tell the opportunities when they come?"

"You can't," the merchant said tartly. "You just have to keep jumping."

Every day presents us with countless opportunities for success in this life and in eternity. More often than not we let them pass, judging them too small to be important. But no situation is unimportant or small if we see it clearly, make proper use of it. If we are spiritually alert, life is a constant progress toward our eternal goal.

Look to yourselves that you do not lose what
we worked for but may receive a full recompense.
2 John 8

O HOLY SPIRIT, MAKE ME AWARE OF EVERY OPPORTUNITY,
EVEN LITTLE THINGS, THAT I MAY DO TO SERVE YOU.

– Works of Mercy –

Social service touches the lives of countless millions. It embraces a wide variety of problems. Child welfare, helping the handicapped and blind to live purposeful lives, restoring confidence to the mentally ill, and encouraging the aged to make good use of their talents are all challenging tasks in this field.

Only comparatively few can devote their lives to professional social work. But everyone can participate in social work on a small scale.

There is not one person who cannot perform, once a day, once a week, once a month, or even once a year, a corporal work of mercy — an act of love to Christ through one of His poor — without any thought of recompense, with no strings attached.

If you can't think of a case which needs your help, check with your church, your doctor, the police department, or with one of many social service agencies. They are in great need of volunteers to assist trained workers, thus releasing them for cases that require more intensive treatment.

> *The aim of this instruction is love from a pure heart,*
> *a good conscience, and a sincere faith.*
> 1 Timothy 1:5

Allow me to play some role, O Lord, in helping
those broken in body or spirit.

– Life Without End –

The word "billion" is a popular one in modem parlance. But have you ever stopped to think what a billion of anything really is?

Perhaps this example will help. If you were a billionaire and decided to give away your money at the rate of $1,000 a day, it would take nearly three years to give away your first million.

But since a billion is one thousand times a million, it would require almost three thousand years to distribute the entire billion.

It is staggering to think in terms of billions of years. Eternity, which you begin the minute you are born, is endless, and a thousand million years from now it will still be in its beginning stages.

Keep ever before you this vast perspective. Life will assume a dynamic, purposeful meaning, and you will gladly endure any earthly sacrifice in order to ensure the happiness God wishes you to enjoy with Him for all eternity.

"For where your treasure is, there also will your heart be."
Matthew 6:21

KEEP MY SIGHTS ON THE ENDLESS YEARS OF ETERNITY, O LORD.

– EIGHT –

Trusting God

One of my favorite parts of being a priest is counseling couples who are preparing for marriage. For most of them, it is a very happy time, even in the midst of the stresses of planning the ceremony and reception. They have a twinkle in their eyes that only grows as the wedding date approaches. For others, the engagement and preparation start off well but become overwhelming, even miserable. The stress tests their relationship in new ways and, in a few sad cases, even breaks them apart.

I love this work because I get a front-row seat to God's wonderful design of marital love, in action, with all of its peaks and valleys, risks and rewards.

Once I get to know the couple well, I ask each partner the following: Do you think your intended spouse would be willing to die for you? With some hesitation, almost everyone says "yes." Then I tell them that, from my experience of guiding many couples, the happiest marriages are the ones in which each spouse is willing to lay down his or her life for the other every single day, in the nitty-gritty realities of their shared existence. This means a decision to seek out the other's preferences, as if they were one's own. It means a habit of prudent deference to the other in decisions about family life, finances, use of free time, and personal goals. I ask them if their intended spouse has proven their willingness and capacity to do this. In other words, are they trustworthy to live for the other?

Marriage to someone unwilling to lay down his or her life for you, both literally and in the humdrum of daily life, is nuts. It is a formula for either divorce or lifelong misery for one or both spouses. On the flip side, if you are blessed to love someone who does sacrifice for you every day, and will continue to do this, then you have found someone worthy of marital trust. When this marital trust is mutual and grounded in truth of action, not just feeling, then marriage resembles the love Christ has for us, his sons and daughters, and for his Church, his spouse.

Similarly, following God must be based on trust. It only makes sense to make a lifetime commitment to Jesus because he is trustworthy. He, the innocent one, died that you and I, sinners, might live forever in heaven, and have life in abundance right now! The perfect man, Jesus Christ, willingly gave up his life, under ridicule, torture, and crucifixion, for our sake — even though we were the ones who necessitated his death with our rebellion and indifference.

Do you trust Jesus in the big things and in the small? Have you committed your life fully to him? Have you made a fundamental life choice for heaven? Are you living according to the commands of God?

It's not so easy, I know. In the following pages Father Keller shows us how.

❧

– An Immeasurable Resource –

One day a small boy was trying to lift a heavy stone, but he couldn't budge it. His father, passing by, stopped to watch his efforts. Finally he said to his son: "Are you using all your strength?"

"Yes, I am," the boy cried, exasperated.

"No," the father said calmly, "you're not. You haven't asked me to help you."

How often we give up when the job seems beyond our limited capacities! And yet we cannot estimate our ability properly, unless we include the immeasurable resource at our disposal when we cooperate with the help of God. When we are attempting a task — big or small — we would do well to stop for a moment and pray, in all humility, for God's help. This is a fitting reminder of our dependence on God, as well as an assurance of help from on high that will carry us through difficulties we could never master alone.

I have the strength for everything through him
who empowers me.
Philippians 4:13

OUR HELP IS IN THE NAME OF THE LORD,
WHO MADE HEAVEN AND EARTH.

– Unless the Lord Builds the House ... –

In 1787, when difficulties arose at the Constitutional Convention in Philadelphia, Benjamin Franklin addressed George Washington, the chairman, in these words:

> The small progress we have made ... is, I think, a melancholy proof of the imperfection of the human understanding.... I have lived, Sir, a long time; and the longer I live, the more convincing proofs I see of this truth, that GOD governs in the affairs of men. And if a sparrow cannot fall to the ground without His notice, is it probable that an empire can rise without His aid? We have been assured, Sir, in the Sacred Writings, that "unless the LORD build the house, they labor in vain who build." I firmly believe this; and I also believe that, without His concurring aid, we shall succeed in this political building no better than the builders of Babel.

The sense of dependence on God that motivated the founders of our country should be a characteristic of every true American today — tomorrow — always!

Unless the Lord build the house,
they labor in vain who build.
Psalm 127:1

O GOD, GRANT THAT WE MAY ALWAYS WORK
TO PRESERVE THE DEMOCRACY THAT IN YOUR
PROVIDENCE YOU HAVE GIVEN US.

– Love Matters Most –

One day when Thomas Aquinas was preaching to the local populace on the love of God, he saw an old woman listening attentively to his every word. And inspired by her eagerness to learn more about her God whom she loved so dearly, he said to the people:

> It is better to be this unlearned woman, loving God with all her heart, than the most learned theologian lacking love.

A great theologian himself, Thomas Aquinas knew that our main avenue of approach to God is love. Though he never belittled knowledge of God — indeed, he wrote volumes monumental in their deep knowledge of the things of God — he insisted on this cardinal point, that if we do not love God and His creatures, our neighbors, and work to increase that love, it matters little how much we know about Him. As Jacques Maritain once said, "Christianity taught man that love is worth more than intelligence."

Whoever is without love does not know God,
for God is love.
1 John 4:8

Jesus, Redeemer who died for me,
give me the love to live for you.

– It's as Good as That –

During a heavy storm at sea, a nervous woman passenger on a large liner went to the captain, seeking reassurance. "Captain," she asked tremulously, "are we in great danger?"

"Don't worry, madam," he answered, "after all, we are in the hands of God."

"Oh," she gasped, terror written on her face, "is it as bad as that?"

We are always in the hands of God, whether or not the weather is stormy. *It's as good as that!* Sometimes we forget God's presence until the last moment, until we feel the storm around us. We should be aware, even during the calm, of the buoying support of Christ.

They came and woke him, saying, "Lord, save us!
We are perishing!" He said to them, "Why
are you terrified, O you of little faith?" Then
he got up, rebuked the winds and the sea, and
there was great calm.
Matthew 8:25-26

IN YOU, O LORD, I PLACE ALL MY HOPE AND TRUST.

– LOOK UP –

Back in the days of sailing ships a young and inexperienced sea-man was sent aloft in a storm to disentangle a length of broken rigging from the mainmast. His body lashed by the raging wind, the youth climbed up swiftly and did the job. As he started down again, he happened to look below him at the angry sea and the rolling deck.

"I'm falling," he shouted, as his grip weakened.

"Don't look down, boy! Look up!" the mate called from the deck below.

The boy forced himself to turn his head and look above him. Calm and reassured, he made his way back to the deck.

If in a panic we decide that we cannot maintain the high level we have achieved, all we need do is look up to God with trust and humility. His arm will steady us.

> LORD *my God, in you I trusted;*
> *save me; rescue me....*
> Psalm 7:2

O LORD, I LOOK TO YOU; KEEP ME STRONG AND SAFE.

– Yes, You Can! –

As the harassed driver approaches an extremely narrow pass on a tortuous road in the Rocky Mountains, he is confronted by the following reassuring sign:

Oh, yes, you can. Millions have.

Sometimes we cannot help but think: "Nobody has ever been as badly off as I am now." When we brood over them, our ills enlarge themselves until they obscure our entire horizon. Yet, if we think of some of the things others have had to suffer, and especially if we remember the unfailing grace of God, our troubles become easier to bear. We realize that it is a part of our human situation to undergo pain, and the eternal reward comes more clearly to mind.

Turn back, Lord, rescue my soul;
save me because of your mercy.
Psalm 6:5

Lord, help me to bear difficulties
bravely for your name's sake.

– UNDER GOD –

The writings of Abraham Lincoln are a rich mine of inspiration. Nearly every speech he made contains evidence of his deep sense of responsibility to God. And it is not hard to see why, since Lincoln himself was constantly seeking higher guidance for his thoughts and actions.

In his famous speech at Baltimore on April 18, 1864, he gave an example of this feeling of dedication when he said: "I am responsible ... to the American people, to the Christian world, to history, and on my final account to God."

An even more famous reference to the Deity occurs in the last sentence of his immortal Gettysburg Address. The initial draft of this speech, however, did not include the words "under God." It was only as he was actually delivering his address that he spontaneously put them in. It was as if he suddenly sensed the incompleteness of his remarks and, with that last and most meaningful addition, gave his speech — and our country — its proper direction:

> ... that this nation, under God, shall have a new birth of freedom — and that government of the people, by the people, for the people, shall not perish from the earth.

My soul longs for your salvation;
I put my hope in your word.
Psalm 119:81

LORD, I RELY ENTIRELY ON YOU, AND I AM RESPONSIBLE
TO YOU FOR ALL MY ACTIONS.

– Declaring Our Interdependence –

Admiral Byrd, on one of his trips to Little America, spent months alone, apart from his party, living in a small cabin equipped with rough furnishings. He had no companion save the fierce Antarctic storms. Single-handed, he cleaned his cabin, checked his instruments, prepared his meals.

One is tempted, reading this, to think that Admiral Byrd was self-sufficient. Yet a little thought reveals how dependent he was upon others. He needed others to get him to Antarctica; to build his cabin; to keep in touch with him by radio. When he was dangerously ill, his men brought him medical aid. He was dependent, too, upon those who financed his project, on the farmers who raised his food, on the designers and manufacturers of his scientific instruments.

One of the weaknesses of our age is that of failing to recognize not only the social nature of man but, even more, man's dependence on God. However, each of us can do his part to restore that recognition, to bring to others the teaching of St. Paul:

None of us lives for oneself,
and no one dies for oneself.
Romans 14:7

O LORD, GRANT THAT WE MAY BEAR WITNESS TO OUR DEPENDENCE
ON OTHER CHRISTIANS AND ULTIMATELY ON YOU.

– Declaration of Dependence –

On July 12, 1775, a year before the signing of the Declaration of Independence, the First Continental Congress issued a solemn proclamation of reliance upon God. It has since become known as the *"Declaration of Dependence."* John Hancock signed it as President of this Congress.

It urged the observance of a special day of prayer for divine guidance in the crisis facing the young nation.

Here are the opening words:

> As the great Governor of the world, by His supreme and universal providence, not only conducts the course of nature with unerring wisdom and rectitude, but frequently influences the minds of men to serve the wise and gracious purposes of His providential government....

Dependence upon Almighty God was an outstanding feature of the beginnings of our great country. It must continue if we are to survive as a free nation.

Those who would undermine our country are champions of atheism. They know they must first remove that *"dependence"* on God before they can enslave us. That should be a challenge for all of us.

> *The fool says in his heart,*
> *"There is no God."*
> Psalm 14:1

AWAKEN US, O JESUS, TO A RENEWED
SENSE OF DEPENDENCE ON YOU.

– "So Help Me God" –

On April 30, 1789, at the Old Federal Building in New York City, George Washington rested his hand on the Holy Bible and took the oath of office as first President of the United States.

According to Joseph Buffington in *The Soul of George Washington* (p. 144), Washington then lifted the Bible to his lips, kissed it, and reverently uttered these four words — "So help me God."

This solemn expression, "So help me God," spontaneously added to the oath by Washington himself, has accompanied official oaths throughout the U.S.A. ever since.

The President taking office, civil service employees, witnesses in all courts, passport applicants, and many others on official occasions repeat these same words. They call on God to be Witness to the truth of what they have solemnly affirmed.

Do whatever you can to keep all Americans conscious of the fact that from its very start our nation has officially recognized our dependence on God; also that each of us is accountable to Him for the manner in which we treat the precious blessing of freedom.

Blessed the man who sets
his security in the LORD.
Psalm 40:5

THANKS TO YOU, ALMIGHTY GOD, FOR YOUR
ABUNDANT GENEROSITY TO OUR LAND.

Conclusion

The Christopher Mission

The letter below is from Father James Keller. It was meant to outline the mission and structure of "The Christophers." In fact, it accomplishes much more than that. It is a prophetic call to all people of goodwill to get involved in the adventure of cultural change, lest the tiny percent of evildoers succeed in radically transforming our nation and world into a godless system. Father Keller explains that this small group of people are united around the cause of ridding the world of the belief that all men and women are created equal by God, and that our human rights, therefore, come from him, not from the state. Have you seen this happen? I have!

This letter needs no further introduction other than to underline how amazingly pertinent a text from the 1950s is for our day. In the six decades since Father Keller wrote this, evil has won many battles, and on the very fronts that Father Keller predicted. This shouldn't discourage us. It should wake us up. I'm certain that if Father Keller were to rewrite the letter today, it would be much the same. People of hope in God's power and mercy know that it is never too late to take up the fight.

I'm not a conspiracy theorist, and I have no idea when the world will come to an end. I do know, however, that you and I are living in our own "end times," as our earthly existence is short. How many years of life do we have in front of us? Between now and then, we are immersed in a battle of eternal consequences. We see around us forces of evil similar to the ones Father Keller pointed to. We also feel the force of our less-than-holy passions leading us to indifference, mediocrity, or even rebellion against God.

171

The Christopher mission today has not changed. We invite you to join a family of people who care. We invite you to do big things, or little things that will make the world a better place. By doing so we are Christ-bearers, the hands and feet of Jesus who still walks among his people doing good.

The Christopher movement is under Catholic auspices. By the very fact that it is Catholic, it is deeply concerned for all time and for eternity with the welfare of *all* men — of Protestants, Jews, those of no formal religion, and those whose background makes them hostile to religion. In loving solicitude we are bound to include *all* and exclude *none*. Each is a child of God at least through creation. Each, doing even one thing for Him, can start to be a Christopher, a Christ-bearer.

Less than 1 percent of humanity has caused most of the world's recent major troubles. This handful — no matter what their labels — mutually shares a militant hatred for the basic truth upon which this nation and all Christian civilization is founded (and without which it cannot endure): that each and every human being shares the common Fatherhood of God, deriving his rights from God, not from the State. Driven by such hatred, those few become missioners of evil, striving to reach the *many*, not merely the *few*. They usually get into one of the four spheres that touch the lives of all people the world over: (1) education, (2) government, (3) labor-management, (4) writing (newspapers, magazines, books, radio, motion pictures, television).

The aim of the Christophers is to get another 1 percent to go as apostolic workers — as Christophers, or Christ-bearers — into the same four fields, and strive at least as hard to *restore* the fundamental truth which the other 1 percent is working furiously to *eliminate*.

It is far more important to get workers of good *in* than it is to get workers of evil *out*. Positive, constructive action is needed.

Little is accomplished by complaining and criticizing: *"It's better to light one candle than to curse the darkness."*

The Christopher movement has *no* chapters, *no* committees, *no* meetings. There are no memberships, no dues. Rather than have a large number of people "paying dues and doing nothing," we have, from the beginning, set out to encourage tens of thousands to "do something and pay nothing." For the material means to carry on the Christopher program our motto is the simple one inscribed on every American coin: "In God We Trust."

God willing, this tiny spark may one day burst into a flame. Fortunately, we have to manufacture nothing; our product is made in heaven. All we have to do is become *distributors* of a changeless Truth in our changing times, ever conscious that there can be neither peace nor freedom without that Truth which "will make you free."

By your living presence as a Christ-bearer in the mainstream of life, you, too, with God's grace, can help renew the face of the earth!

— Father James Keller, M.M.

The Christophers

Father James Keller, M.M., founded The Christophers in 1945 with the goal of using media (print, radio, and TV) to help people discover their God-given talents and use them for the greater good. Since that time, we have been spreading this simple yet profound Gospel-based message. In 2015, we celebrated the seventieth anniversary year of our organization, and our mission is still going strong.

Our News Notes, prayer cards, and "Three Minutes a Day" books are widely disseminated among those on the front lines of the toughest ministries, such as prisons and hospitals. Our annual Christopher Awards recognize the best the world has to offer in books, films, and television programs that affirm the highest values of the human spirit.

Our weekly "Christopher Closeup" radio show, featuring guests who reflect the ideals of lighting a candle rather than cursing the darkness, airs on SiriusXM's The Catholic Channel, the Relevant Radio network, and numerous other stations around the country. In addition, Communications Director Tony Rossi shares podcasts and articles about his interviews on our blog along with a wide range of insights on culture and important events of the day.

The Christophers' annual video contest for college students and poster contest for high school students ignite a spark in young people that encourages them to utilize their creativity for the expression of beauty and truth, helping ensure that the next generation of communicators will bring light into the world. And Father Jonathan Morris hosts The Christophers' video series exploring practical approaches to life's most complex problems.

To be a Christopher is to answer the call to reach out to others in a spirit of kindness, to explore our own unique purpose in life, and to join with people of goodwill in bringing light and hope to all. For more information, visit www.christophers.org.